A Texas Christmas

Written and Compiled by
MARILYN COVINGTON

Foreword by
JANICE WOODS WINDLE

Photography by
RICHARD REYNOLDS

WESTCLIFFE PUBLISHERS

ENGLEWOOD, COLORADO

EDITOR: Kristen Iversen
DESIGNER: Rebecca Finkel, F + P Graphic Design
PRODUCTION MANAGER: Craig Keyzer

TEXT
© 1999 Marilyn Covington.
ALL RIGHTS RESERVED.

PHOTOGRAPHY
© 1999 Richard Reynolds. ALL RIGHTS RESERVED.

INTERNATIONAL STANDARD BOOK NUMBER
1-56579-344-7

LIBRARY OF CONGRESS
CATALOGING-IN-PUBLICATION
Covington, Marilyn, 1945–
   A Texas Christmas / text by Marilyn
Covington ; photography by Richard
Reynolds.
   p. cm.
   ISBN 1-56579-344-7
   1. Christmas—Texas. 2. Texas—
Social life and customs.
   I. Title.
GT4986.T4C68 1999   99-23652
394.2663'097643—dc21   CIP

PUBLISHER
Westcliffe Publishers, Inc.
P.O. Box 1261
Englewood, Colorado 80150

PRINTED IN HONG KONG
THROUGH WORLD PRINT, LTD.

*For information about other fine books and
calendars from Westcliffe Publishers, please contact
your local bookstore, contact us at 1-800-523-3692,
write for our free color catalog, or visit our website
at www.westcliffepublishers.com.*

*FIRST OVERLEAF: Agave and juniper tree in
Big Bend National Park*
*SECOND OVERLEAF: A striking chili pepper/barbed
wire wreath along the Salado Stroll*

*I WOULD LIKE TO EXPRESS SPECIAL THANKS TO:
My husband George, who has traveled many miles with me and supported
and encouraged me when the trail got bumpy.*

*My daughter Laurie, who spent countless hours researching, proofreading,
and tabulating taste test results and still managed to finish her master's degree.*

*My friend Jane Clancy Debenport — the Texas half of my brain — who
aided, abetted, and prodded this effort from day one.*

*To friends and neighbors Ann Buchmann and Ellen Earle, for their constant
support and willingness to tackle the enormous job of testing the recipes.*

TABLE OF CONTENTS

Texas-style Christmas cheer

FOREWORD

The Night Saint Nickolaus Fell off the Roof

by Janice Woods Windle

My mother, Virginia Bergfeld Woods, still lives in the house which for 113 years has been the family homeplace on Court Street in Seguin, Texas. Mother is a phenomenal storyteller and our family treasure. My favorite Christmas story—now that I have renewed my faith in Santa Claus and in his predecessor, Saint Nickolaus (perhaps they're the same)—is about her memory of St. Nickolaus Eve. I know only that St. Nickolaus Eve is an old German custom observed at the end of the first week in December. Its celebration is like an exclamation point and will prepare you for the wonderful Christmas observances that follow, but I will let Mother tell you the story as she has told me and my children so often:

There was a time when parents could unashamedly discipline their children with a little bribe and never think twice about a Dr. Benjamin Spock.

"Now, if you are good little girls," my daddy would say, with a broad smile, "you will have a peppermint candy cane or perhaps an apple in your stocking when you wake up in the morning. Or maybe candy will come tumbling down the chimney from St. Nickolaus."

And then he added, losing his smile and shaking his finger at my older sister Mary-Louise and me—even at Maxine, my toddler sister, "Or *(ominous pause)* if you're naughty, St. Nickolaus will put switches in your stocking—see that peach tree right outside the window?—cut from that very tree. And *(ominous pause)* you know what that means!"

Although Daddy looked formidable, a little glint in his eye must have told me there would be no switch—never was and never would be — but I vowed to be extra, extra good, just in case. My mama appeared to be suppressing a giggle for some reason. I figured it out only years later, you know.

The most memorable St. Nickolaus Eve occurred in 1919. I was not quite six. It was shortly after Uncle Max Bergfeld, my father Will Bergfeld's brother, visited us after serving in Europe in World War I. Uncle Max was a handsome, tall, happy-go-lucky young man, and so agile he must have brought forth a little envy from my father. He would play with us girls, hoist us into trees, and push us so high in our swings (bringing screams of terror from my mother), and he could run footraces that left everyone else panting behind.

But what was the most fun was that he could twirl a cowboy rope and capture tree trunks (and little girls) with a single toss—just like Tom Mix in the movies!

When St. Nickolaus Eve arrived, the suggestion—probably coming from Uncle Max himself—that he go up on the roof and make a noise so St. Nickolaus's arrival would seem more real to his nieces was probably irresistible to my parents, especially to my fun-loving father. After "St. Nickolaus" made a tremendous noise, stomping around on the roof, he would fling candy and lollipops down the fireless chimney. I'm sure now it was an offer not even my mother could resist.

"Please be careful, Max," I know she would have warned. "Shingles can be very slippery, especially at night when the dew falls."

On this particular St. Nickolaus Eve, we began by singing carols. Daddy, Uncle Max, and Grandpa Bergfeld played their violins and Mama played the piano.

For some strange reason Uncle Max put down his violin and said he had to leave—right in the middle of things!

I remember that terrible thump and rumble noise—vividly. It must have been late because, in spite of all the excitement and expectation, my sisters and I were sound asleep. When I think of it now, I am sure I heard the midnight bells from the hall clock even as I heard the stomp of heavy steps on the roof. Then I heard a yell followed by a great clatter and running within the house as Mother screamed, Daddy yelled, and doors slammed open and shut.

Like a jack-in-the-box, we girls popped up from beneath our bedcovers.

Then, as they did in Samuel Clement's famous poem: We sprang from our bed to see what was the matter!

And down the hall we flew. Our bare feet skipped across the cold oak floor. Our flannel nighties flapped around our ankles.

Baby Maxine called after us, "Me too, me too!" and clambered out of her crib.

When what to our wondering eyes should appear? But Uncle Max sprawled flat upon the ground!

I backed up for a better view of the roof—especially the chimney. Could St. Nickolaus still be there?

When I learned he was gone, I whirled on my uncle who was sitting up and rubbing his head. I stuck my angry little face close to his. "Uncle Max, you bad, bad, man! You tried to rope St. Nick, didn't you?" Even at that tender age, I knew about the mischievous Bergfeld men and their practical jokes.

Uncle Max's mouth curled, anticipating a hearty laugh.

His merry eyes looked into mine and gave a long wink.

"Hey, kiddo, tell me something. You girls get any switches in your stockings tonight?" he asked.

Watercolor by Jerry Weers

In actuality we had five Christmas celebrations: St. Nickolaus Eve, Christmas Eve, Christmas morning, Christmas dinner, and, finally, Christmas night at the Methodist Church.

We hung our stockings individually on chairs around our potbellied stove. Gifts included underwear made from flour sacks with tiny buttons and hand-sewn buttonholes. Once I got a beautiful porcelain doll imported from Germany, dressed in white with delicate lace trim. It was even more special because it had real hair and, wonder of wonders, eyes that opened and closed.

Christmas dinner was typically Texan. Candied sweet potatoes, chicken or turkey, luscious gravy, spiced peaches, biscuits or cornbread, and fruitcake, but we children could hardly eat we were so anxious to see the Christmas tree in the living room just behind closed double doors into the parlor. Those doors had remained closed far too long for us and there was no peeking allowed.

Well, there was no peeking until each of the children recited a poem or verse. I still remember mine:

> I like cake, I like pie,
> I like a little boy about this high.
> Now, Mommy, you just hold your tongue
> 'cause you liked little boys when you were young!

When the last verse was recited, the double doors into the parlor were opened. And what a sight it was! The green pine tree stood directly under the chandelier in the middle of the room. It had no candles, but light from the chandelier made the German crystal ornaments shimmer a glistening light on the Santa Claus figures, the tiny silver bells, and the white frosted reindeer.

As long as I live, I will never forget those beautiful, beautiful trees. And neither will I forget the feeling of warmth and security, of love and friendship from parents and grandparents, uncles, aunts, and cousins. One special gift I often reflect upon is the quarter each of us received from Great-Grandpa Moss.

That twenty-five cents was good for five matinees at the Palace Theater, where we could see Rudolph Valentino riding across the desert, Mary Pickford pleading for mercy from a villain, Pearl White tied to a railroad track with an oncoming train in the distance, and, best of all, Tom Mix twirling a rope—just like my Uncle Max.

May this beautiful book bring you the joy of Christmas memories. May turning its pages inspire you to create your own stories for future generations.

Janice Woods Windle

Janice Woods Windle

With special thanks to the Sophienburg Museum in New Braunfels and the Seguin Conservation Society.

Janice Woods Windle is the author of TRUE WOMEN (1994) and HILL COUNTRY (1998) and president of the El Paso Community Foundation.

Quick Reference

Fort Worth—old and new—edged in sparkling Christmas lights

PREFACE

"The stars at night are BIG and BRIGHT..." but they sure have serious competition during the holiday season, *"Deep in the heart of Texas!"* Millions and millions of lights sparkle from buildings, houses, trees, boats, lamp posts, pump jacks, oil derricks, tumbleweeds, and even cars and pickup trucks, transforming this Lone Star State into an incomparable galaxy of twinkling holiday spirit. Everything, including Christmas, I learned as I crisscrossed this state, is BIGGER and BETTER in Texas.

In my eighteen years as a Texan, I've heard it said that "Texas is a whole 'nother country." But after traveling over six thousand miles (without ever leaving the state), I can unequivocally say that "Texas is about six other countries!" I think as I started my journey to find Christmas in Texas, I felt much like I imagine Coronado did as he set off to search for the legendary Seven Cities of Cibola—excited by the stories of the gleaming golden cities; spurred on by the lure of the unknown; and scared those around him would realize he didn't have a clue where he was going!

Well, "go" became the most operative verb in my vocabulary. I loaded my car with 40 pounds of maps and guidebooks and took to the Texas highways and byways in search of Christmas. I explored the wealth of German traditions in the Hill Country, Czech traditions in Central Texas, and Hispanic traditions throughout South Texas and beyond. I reveled in the history of East Texas and gained new appreciation for the rugged West Texas frontier. But most of all, I listened to the people all across Texas who stopped and talked with me, sharing their enormous pride in local traditions and celebrations. They spun nostalgic Christmas stories, sang me songs, and bragged of favorite family holiday recipes. They welcomed me with enthusiasm into their historic homes and museums. Everywhere I went, I felt like an honored guest at a big family reunion. Christmas, it seems, is the universal key that unlocks the wondrous door to remembrance of family and happy times while also opening a sun roof of Texas community pride that shouts to the heavens, "As big as it was last year, it's gonna be twice as BIG this year!"

The lighted Christmas Parade in Marshall

Like Coronado, I searched for "glittering" cities, but my search, unlike his, bore fruit far beyond my expectations. Amidst the galaxy of glittering lights and displays, I found a proud state that truly knows how to celebrate its richly diverse cultural and historical heritage. I found communities overflowing with enormous holiday spirit. But more importantly, I discovered the source of Texas's greatest treasure—the people strung across this great state like strands of living holiday lights who share their warmth and glow all year round. I hope we have been able to capture at least a part of this "glow" to brighten your holidays with a Texas-sized Christmas spirit that knows no bounds.

Merry Christmas, Y'all!

Marilyn Covington

*Dedicated with love to my
family and friends, both old
and new, all across Texas who
opened their hearts and homes
and shared their wealth of
Christmas experiences.*

— MC

Heavily laden tree at House of the Seasons in Jefferson

Reflections of Christmas Past

¡FELIZ NAVIDAD! FRÖHE WEINACHTEN! JOYEUX NOËL! VESELÉ VÁNOCE! No matter how they say "Merry Christmas, Y'all," Texans come together at Christmas and set the Lone Star State aglow with a unique blend of cultures and traditions—and Texans DO love tradition almost as much as they love celebrating! Through religious festivals, historical reenactments, songs, strolls, Victorian candlelight tours, and above all lights, billions of lights, the people of Texas ring in this season of joy with an abiding sense of continuation from their cultural origins.

From the tightly woven fabric of the history of Mexico and Texas come some of the state's most colorful holiday traditions. *La Fiesta de las Luminarias* (Festival of Lights) combines Old World Spanish traditions with New World interpretations for glorious celebrations ablaze with glowing lights. Luminarias (lighted candles placed in sand-weighted paper sacks) symbolically show the way for Mary and Joseph as they journey to Bethlehem, and are also thought to lead the Magi to the baby Jesus. During *La Fiesta de las Luminarias* in San Antonio, 2,500 luminarias line the walkways of the Paseo del Rio (The Riverwalk) the first three weekends in December, lighting the way for thousands of holiday visitors.

Christmas activities "lasted more than a fortnight" in the ranch country around Junction, an English woman, Mary J. Jaques, wrote in Texas Ranch Life *in 1890. She described horse races "of an amusingly, non-descript character—horses, ponies of all ages and sizes, carrying any weight and ridden with or without saddle . . ." and a "dexterous feat is to pick up a hat, a handkerchief or even a dollar, from the ground at full gallop."*

Opposite: The Faust House in New Braunfels
Overleaf: A dramatic view of winter in Big Bend National Park

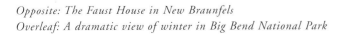

Choral voices arching over the river lend magic to San Antonio's Posada

Las Posadas

Each Christmas in El Paso, Goliad, San Antonio, and countless other communities around the state, Hispanic Texans carry on the ancient tradition of *Las Posadas* (The Lodgings), reenacting the journey of Mary and Joseph in search of shelter on the night of Jesus' birth. Spanish missionaries in the sixteenth century first brought this expressive religious drama to Texas to teach the Indians about the birth of Christ. Today, the holiday celebration begins nine days before Christmas with the solemnity of the candlelight *posada* processions followed by lively, music-filled parties.

Every parish, community, or neighborhood brings its own unique sense of pageantry to *Las Posadas.* In 1966, the San Antonio Conservation Society began what has become the state's largest annual interpretation of this rich and colorful celebration. Set against the glittering backdrop of the Riverwalk, children, costumed as shepherds, angels, Mary, and Joseph, lead the huge, candlelight procession along the winding pathways of luminarias. Along the way, choirs and mariachis fill the air with traditional *posada* songs.

Soon, the candle bearers stop and sing the age-old plea for lodging:

> *En el nombre del ceilo os pido posada.*
> [In the name of heaven I ask for housing.]
>
> *pues no puede andar ya me esposa amada.*
> [My beloved wife is no longer able to travel.]

Carolers representing the innkeepers send them on their way with:

> *¡¡Aquí no es mesón!! ¡Sigan adelante!*
> [No room here. Go on ahead!]
>
> *Pues no puedo abrir. No sea algún tunante.*
> [I cannot open. Don't be stubborn.]

Sadly the children trudge onward along the path of glowing luminarias. Twice they stop and are turned away, and twice the procession continues on until they reach the humble stable at La Villita's Arneson River Theater, where they finally hear the joyous words:

> *Entren, Santos Peregrinos, y reciban éste rincón,*
> [Enter, holy pilgrims, And take your corner,]
>
> *no de esta pobre morado sino de mi corazon . . .*
> [Not in my poor house, But in my heart. . .]

Once the pageant is over and the candles extinguished, the joyous celebrations begin in nearby Maverick Plaza in true Mexican style with lively mariachi music and dancing, refreshments of hot chocolate and cookies, and the children's perennial favorite—bashing brightly colored piñatas until the candy, peanuts, and other tantalizing surprises shower down into the scramble of waiting hands.

Other interpretations of *Las Posadas* may take the more ancient form of a novena with nine families participating in the ritual processions. One family begins the traditional journey nine nights before Christmas, stopping to ask for lodging at the home of the next family. As in the above version, entrance is denied and the family continues along a luminaria-lit path, joined by each successive family until they reach the ninth house. There they gain *posada* and are invited in for refreshments. This ritual continues each night until Christmas Eve, when each of the nine families has served as host. This last "night of nights," the most elaborate party of the week, follows the conclusion of the procession.

No matter how large or small the celebration, the *posada* message goes far beyond the reenactment of the original holy journey. It offers participants and spectators alike an opportunity to find "room" in their hearts for the true spirit of Christmas, and it also spans the generations, passing down to the young a sense of connection to the richness of their Hispanic heritage.

No party is complete for Hispanic children without piñata breaking. An old tradition says it is symbolic of beating away the devil by the innocent faith of children.

—**MARILYN COVINGTON**

Las Posadas procession on Paseo del Rio, San Antonio

Los Pastores

Another Christmas tradition passed down through the generations from Spain to Mexico to Texas is the medieval mystery play *Los Pastores* (The Shepherds). After Christmas each year since 1945, the Guadalupe Players perform the San Antonio Conservation Society's

presentation of *Los Pastores* at Mission San José. This partly serious, partly comic pageant depicts the primal struggle between good and evil through the story of the shepherds' journey to pay homage to the baby Jesus. The audience suffers along with the shepherds as they are distracted by all-too-human impulses; then, the watchers scream in dismay as Lucifer springs out of Hell to tempt and torment the shepherds. Good skirmishes with evil over and over until St. Michael finally appears and defeats the devil with a powerful blow; then, the shepherds joyfully complete their journey and place their gifts before the Christ Child.

Sitting on the grounds of the mission amidst glowing luminarias, the audience can readily imagine how the native Indians must have watched in awe as the early Franciscan friars acted out the story of the shepherds. *Los Pastores,* performed in Spanish with English narration, gives visitors a rare opportunity to see one of the few medieval plays still regularly performed in this country.

Mission San Jose y San Miguel de Aguayo, San Antonio

Christmas Eve Feast

Christmas Eve, in Hispanic Texan households, means feasting. Menus may vary from family to family with tortilla or taco soup, enchiladas, chicken mole, cornbread, pico de gallo, guacamole, or maybe even a bowl of red, hot chili, but all agree that the most delectable Hispanic holiday tradition to grace any fiesta table is the tamale. "It just wouldn't be Christmas Eve without tamales" is the refrain heard round the Lone Star State! Tamale recipes, however, tend to be well-guarded, family secrets handed down from generation to generation. "Tamale making . . . is not a recipe, but an enthusiastic joint effort of food preparation . . . the heart and soul of the holiday season," writes Anne Lindsay Greer in *Cuisine of the American Southwest.* Hispanic women make large quantities of tamales during the Christmas holidays—some use pork roasts, but traditionally hog's heads are used. Tamales are in such demand for Christmas Eve that families not making their own usually place an order with their favorite tamale maker weeks in advance. Sweet tamales (made with fruit or nut centers), Buñuelos, or Reposteria (Mexican sugar cookies), along with a steaming mug of Mexican Chocolate, usually finish the festive Christmas Eve party fare with a delicious flare.

TAMALES

3 ¼ lb. pork roast (small bone)
3 ¼ lb. beef roast
2 ½ lb. lard or Crisco
2 tsp. ground comino seed

1 tsp. black pepper
1 whole bulb garlic, minced
2 bay leaves
1 red chili pod—dried, soaked, and seeds removed
1 (3 oz.) bottle chili powder (or more, if desired)

½ cup salt to taste
1 ½ lb. dried corn shucks
7 ½ lb. Masa (prepared Masa can be bought ready-made)

Place roasts in kettle with bay leaves, cover with water, and boil until roasts are tender. Reserve the broth, grind meat with meat grinder, or mince. Melt 1/2 lb. lard in large kettle and combine with ground meats; mix together well. In a small pot add two cups of water, take seeds out of chili pod, boil for 10 minutes or so. Add to the ground meat. Mix chili pod (ground), comino, black pepper, garlic, half the jar of chili powder, 1 to 2 Tbsp. salt; stir until all ingredients are well mixed. If the mixture is too dry, add reserved broth until moist. Simmer 20 minutes, uncovered, until flavors are absorbed. Skim off any excess grease and reserve to use with the Masa. Soak 1 ½ lb. corn shucks in warm water in a large dishpan to soften, overnight if desired. Rinse 2 or 3 times to remove any corn silks. Blot dry on paper towels or on drainboard to drain excess water. If corn shucks are large, cut them on top or in half.

Divide Masa in half. To half the Masa, work in lard, ¼ lb. at a time, until 1 lb. has been added. Add ⅛ bottle of chili powder, ¼ cup salt or less. Mix by hand until ingredients are well blended. Put aside and repeat, using the remaining half of ingredients. Add broth to Masa mixtures and mix with your hands until Masa is a spreadable paste. Using knife or back of spoon, spread a thin layer of Masa on the smooth side of the corn shucks. Place 2 to 3 Tbsp. of the meat mixture on each shuck. Roll the corn shuck like a cigarette, then fold over the top of the shuck to keep the filling from falling out while cooking. Leave the bottom of the tamale open.

Using a tamale can, put corn shucks in the bottom, tie with corn shuck strings, 4 tamales, make it in a pyramid fashion. Add broth to a depth of several inches. Fill the kettle with tamales, standing at a slant with open end up so the filling will not fall out. Cover the top with empty corn shucks, and a very clean cheesecloth or foil. Cover and steam over medium heat for 1 hour. Add more broth if needed. The Masa will be firm, but not dry when tamales are done. Tamales are to your taste—mild or hot.

Makes 19 to 20 dozen. Add variations—if Masa is left over, use refried beans/hot peppers or chicken, seasoned; or raisin, dates, cinnamon, pecan mixture, then add sugar to taste to Masa.

—HORTENSIA B. HERNANDEZ
(from *Holiday Reflections Cook Book*)
used by permission from Sophienburg Museum and Archives—New Braunfels

MEXICAN CHOCOLATE

10 gallons milk

20 tablets Mexican chocolate

1 32 oz. can Nestlé Quick Instant
   Chocolate

4 packages cinnamon sticks

5 lb. white sugar

Boil chocolate slowly over low heat, in just enough water to cover it, until it dissolves. Add cinnamon sticks, stir very often. Add milk and Nestlé Chocolate. Add sugar and taste, adding more if needed. Serves 100.

SMALL RECIPE: *(Follow directions above. Serves 25.)*

2½ gallons milk

5 tablets Mexican chocolate

8 oz. Nestlé Quick Instant Chocolate

1 package cinnamon sticks

1¼ lb. white sugar

—**MRS. VIDALA H. CASTILLEJA**
(from *Holiday Reflections Cook Book*)
used by permission from Sophienburg Museum and Archives—New Braunfels

REPOSTERIA (Mexican Sugar Cookies)

5 cups flour

4 sticks margarine (1 lb.)

2 Tbsp. Crisco shortening

3 tsp. vanilla

1 cup sugar

Sprinkles

½ cup sugar—divide and add blue
   and red food coloring

¼ cup sugar on flat plate for dipping glass

Mix ingredients and blend until smooth. Shape into small balls, about walnut size. Place on ungreased cookie sheet and flatten with bottom of glass dipped in sugar. Sprinkle with bright-colored sugar (blue or red). Bake at 375° F for 15 minutes or until light golden brown.

Very colorful during the holiday season!

—**MONICA CHABESTE**
(from *Holiday Reflections Cook Book*)
used by permission from Sophienburg Museum and Archives—New Braunfels

TACO SOUP

1½ lb. hamburger

1 large onion, chopped

1 package taco mix

1 package Hidden Valley original ranch
   salad dressing mix

1 15.5 oz. can kidney beans

1 15 oz. can pinto beans with jalapeno

1 10 oz. can Rotel tomatoes w/green chilis

1 15.5 oz. can yellow hominy

2 14.5 oz. cans tomatoes

Brown hamburger and onion. Add rest of ingredients; do not drain. Simmer for 30 minutes.

—**PATTI KIMBERLIN,** *Missouri City*

A festive Christmas Eve table laden with tamales, pico de gallo, venison chili, and chili con queso

MEXICAN CORN BREAD

1 cup yellow cornmeal	2 eggs	1 cup grated cheddar cheese
½ tsp. salt	1 cup milk	3 to 5 seeded chopped
1 heaping Tbsp. flour	1 cup chopped onion	jalapenos
½ tsp. baking soda	3 or 4 garlic cloves	
⅓ cup oil	1 can cream-style corn	

Mix dry ingredients. Add oil, eggs, and milk. Stir in rest of ingredients and pour into greased skillet. Bake at 350° for 1 hour or longer if needed.

—**PATTI KIMBERLIN,** *Missouri City*

HOLIDAY TORTILLA CHIPS

1 cup masa harina	½ tsp. salt
4 oz. water	vegetable oil
30 drops food coloring	

Heat vegetable oil ½ inch deep in a medium saucepan. Combine food coloring and water. Place flour in mixing bowl and gradually add water mixture until a firm dough is achieved. Knead for 2 minutes and let stand for 5 minutes. Place dough on a cutting board between two sheets of wax paper. With a rolling pin, roll out to a thickness of about ⅛ inch. Remove top sheet and cut out shapes with cookie cutters. Lift chips with a spatula, and gently place into hot oil. Cook for about 60 seconds, turning over several times. Makes 15–20 chips.

—**RICHARD REYNOLDS,** *Austin*

German Traditions

In the mid 1800s, right before Texas achieved statehood, German pioneers made their way into the central part of Texas, bringing with them many of the holiday customs that have become synonymous with today's American and Texan Christmas celebrations. The German Tannenbaum (Christmas tree), the advent wreath, decorating with mistletoe (which grew here plentifully, much to the delight of the early settlers), and familiar carols like "Silent Night" are now a standard part of our holidays thanks to those hardy settlers who were able to adapt the Old Country customs to the Texas wilderness conditions.

Christmas Tree Forest during Weihnachten in Fredericksburg

Early German immigrants, not finding their traditional fir trees available, decorated Texas cedar and juniper trees (and sometimes even oak or peach trees) with fruits, nuts, homemade cookies, chains of colored paper, and strings of berries. Parents decorated the tree in secret, putting presents under the tree and decorating the room. On Christmas Eve, with the much anticipated lighting of the tree's candles, the children were allowed to enter and see the shining tree for the first time. Children watched the tree in awe, hoping to be the one to find the pickle hidden in the branches. According to tradition, the child who spots the pickle first gets an extra surprise.

Christmas Eve is also the traditional time for opening presents and feasting on Christmas goose in German households. Early settlers sometimes had to settle for wild turkey when goose was scarce, but whatever the main course, there is always a plentiful array of special foods on the German holiday table—herring salad (for good luck), *Lebkuchen* (honey cakes), Marzipan, *Pfeffernüsse* (peppernut) cookies, and *weiss Kuchen mit Frucht* (fruitcake).

Composed in Germany on Christmas Eve in 1818, "Silent Night," one of the world's most beloved carols, is still sung in German throughout much of Central Texas. "Every year," reports Judy Young of New Braunfels, "our city has a community get-together. We gather and sing traditional carols, ending up in front of historic First Protestant Church, where we light our candles and sing all the verses of 'Stille Nacht' in German. During the hush that follows the last note, there is such an amazing feeling of oneness—that's what says 'Christmas' to me."

A German turkey feather tree and miniature village at Sam Houston Park, Houston

On *Zweite Weihnachten* (Second Christmas), which is celebrated the day after Christmas, Germans leave behind the serious nature of the religious observances and kick up their heels at community dances and parties. In Fredericksburg, members of the historical society get together each December 26 for a feast of German holiday foods and old-fashioned singing and dancing—as much fun today as it was 150 years ago!

Stille Nacht, Heilige Nacht
SILENT NIGHT, HOLY NIGHT

Melodie: Franz Gruber (1818)
Text: Joseph Mohr (1818)

1. Stil - le Nacht, hei - li - ge Nacht! Al - les schläft, ein - sam wacht

nur das trau - te hoch - hei - li - ge Paar. Hol - der Kna - be im lok - ki - gen Haar,

schlaf in himm - li - scher Ruh, _____ schlaf in himm - li - scher Ruh! _____

Satz: W. Gohl

Silent night, holy night,
All is calm, all is bright
Round yon virgin mother and child
Holy infant so tender and mild,
Sleep in heavenly peace.

Silent night, holy night,
Shepherds quake at the sight
Glories stream from heaven afar,
Heavenly host sing alleluia;
Christ, the Savior, is born!

Silent night, holy night,
Son of God, love's pure light
Radiant beams from thy holy face,
With the dawn of redeeming grace,
Jesus, Lord, at thy birth.

Christmas in Fredericksburg

by Debbie Smithdeal

Located in the heart of the Texas Hill Country, Fredericksburg is thought of by many Texans to be in God's country. Lush rolling hills and rich soil attracted German immigrants to this area over 150 years ago. While Christmas is a special time of year all over Texas, it seems even more so to a quaint town so richly blessed with German heritage.

The Kammlah House and Store, circa 1849, Pioneer Museum Complex, Fredericksburg

Shortly after Thanksgiving, thousands of twinkling lights adorn Fredericksburg's historic buildings, trees, and shrubs along Main Street. Music, food, and traditions handed down from German pioneers are brought out to be enjoyed by residents and visitors alike. This season offers a feast for the eyes as well as the palate, the nose, and the ears.

On the first Friday in December, the Christmas season is ushered in by a parade down Main Street, culminating in an annual tree-lighting ceremony and the much-heralded arrival of St. Nicholas. This begins Weihnachten, a ten-day celebration at Marketplatz (town square) featuring food, music, and crafts fashioned after marketplaces of yesteryear. One example of local artistry is the Christmas tree forest, with uniquely beautiful trees decorated by local charitable organizations. The fully decorated trees are individually auctioned, to then adorn the homes of lucky bidders.

During the second weekend in December, the Gillespie County Historical Society grounds are transformed with Christmas finery. The Fredericksburg Theater Company performs "A Step Back in Time," a reenactment of historic Christmases in Fredericksburg. The site comes alive with strolling carolers in authentic period attire, trees laden with twinkling lights, and steaming cups of wassail poured before an aromatic bonfire. Time-travel guides usher small groups of visitors into assorted historic buildings to view musical and theatrical vignettes as they might have been presented nearly a hundred years ago. The program concludes with a musical review performed in an 1855 Greek Revival chapel dressed in candle-light and Christmas greenery. Succulent seasonal desserts and beverages ensure that no one leaves without a healthy helping of Christmas spirit.

The following evening, the Historical Society sponsors a candlelight tour of approximately twenty architecturally unique homes and buildings erected from the early 1800s to the present day. (Most are either designed, constructed, or heavily influenced by early German craftsmen.) Dressed in Christmas finery and filled with aromas and music of Christmas, each building or home seems more beautiful than the one before.

If Walt Disney and Norman Rockwell had conspired to select the perfect town to epitomize Christmas in Texas, they would surely have agreed on Fredericksburg. Good cheer permeates the air and lightens the hearts of all who are fortunate enough to share its holiday blessings.

When my husband was stationed in Germany with the U.S. Army, our son, Jack, was only about three weeks old. We had his picture taken on the base with Santa Claus and then with the German St. Nickolaus—we enjoyed both Texas and German traditions that Christmas.

—JESSICA HUDDLESTON WILDS, *Temple*

EXCERPTS FROM "MEMOIR OF A TEXAS CHRISTMAS"

WRITTEN IN 1894 *by William Andreas Trenckmann*

I first heard of the coming of Christmas on a rainy October day [1863]—I was at that time a tow-headed little fellow of four, the pampered youngest child of the family. I was watching the passageway with curiosity as hams, sausages and bacon, woolen stockings, shirts and underclothes and—most welcome of all—enormous rolls of tobacco were being carefully sewn into packages and labeled. "For Christmas for your brothers in the war!" was the answer to my question about the destination of all these fine things. "For Christmas!" These words were enough to awaken in my little head the slumbering memory of the splendors of the past Christmas. From now on I did nothing but pester my mother to tell me about Santa Claus and Christmas . . . .

During the week before the celebration all kinds of strange experiments were carried out in the kitchen; since I could not very well be banished from the kitchen because of the prevailing wet weather, I was allowed to watch most of them. The problem was how to bake cookies for the Christmas tree without wheat flour, without raisins and almonds and all of the usual ingredients. And indeed the baking was successfully accomplished with finely ground corn meal and honey; instead of almonds and raisins, scalded peach kernels and shelled pecans were used for decoration. To us the cookies tasted splendid, but they had the disadvantage of being very brittle, and these little stars and animal figures soon fell from the tree. Concerning the candles for the tree, however, we were better off than we are today, for they were carefully molded of beeswax . . . .

[Christmas Day] Hardly had dusk arrived when the supper bell rang. I don't have much to report about the evening meal, since of course I was so excited that I couldn't get a bite down. This much I still recall, that on that evening, in honor of the event, instead of the usual prairie tea, coffee was drunk—not acorn, grain, or sweet-potato coffee, but coffee made from genuine freshly roasted beans that had just been shipped in. The main attraction of the meal however was an enormous wild tom turkey, which our cousin had killed the day before from his bedroom window . . . .

Finally, finally: the longed-for ringing of the bell from the main house! In the greatest hurry we dashed through the dark passageway; on the porch, which was slicked over with ice, all three of us lost our footing and I hit my head against a post . . . . Our parents quickly opened the door, helped us safely back onto our feet, and now we plunged breathlessly into the room. I for my part had eyes only for the Christmas tree for quite some time. It was a beautiful, slender young wild peach tree that reached to the ceiling. For decorations they had used red berries from the woods, the Christmas cookies that had been so laboriously produced, and nuts in little baskets of colored paper. There were also candy sticks on the tree, but they had been made of brown Louisiana sugar and were not much to look at . . . but two gigantic golden-yellow oranges, which my father had brought back from his trip, were the most marvelous thing on the whole tree. All these splendors stood out all the more strikingly against the dark, shiny deep green of the wild peach tree, in which the numerous candles were reflected.

ENGLISH TRANSLATION FROM BELLVILLE HISTORICAL SOCIETY ARCHIVES

William Trenckmann started DAS BELLVILLE WOCHENBLATT, a weekly newspaper, in 1891. It was published in Bellville and intended for the neighboring Texas-German communities in which English was still a second language. This memoir appeared in Wochenblatt Kalender für 1894/Beilage zu No. 11 des Bellville Wochenblatt.

Miniature historic scene nestled under the boughs of the Timmermann sisters' festive Tannenbaum in Geronimo

The Seven Timmermann Sisters

Over half a century ago, the seven Timmermann sisters in the tiny town of Geronimo, near Seguin, began their tradition of sharing the spirit of traditional German Christmases with the community. From decorating a huge cedar tree with German-style cookies, fruit, and antique family ornaments to creating an elaborate, miniature reproduction of an early New Braunfels German Christmas, the Timmermann sisters transform their 1893 family farmhouse into a living classroom of traditions and memories for all who visit during the holidays. The miniature scene under the tree, based on diary descriptions written in 1849 by teacher Hermann Seele, has delighted thousands of visiting school children with its intricate details—even running water for the Guadalupe River!

It's German tradition to hide a pickle in the branches of the tree. The child who finds it gets an extra surprise.

Through the years the Timmermanns have received national recognition through many feature articles in magazines and newspapers and have also made several television appearances. In 1963, they also had the privilege of being asked to bake cookies for President and Mrs. Johnson's Christmas tree; they made a Papa Johnson cookie for the president, a cardinal for Lady Bird Johnson, and additional cookies for other members of the family as well as a visiting ambassador.

Today, although only two of the sisters are living, they continue in their lifelong vocation of sharing the old German ways with the young by sponsoring scholarships through sales of their book of reminiscences and recipes: *As We Remember . . . Bread Pudding & Wine Sauce*. From this book comes the following description:

> *And on our Christmas Tree, among the fragile ornaments, the apples*
> *and oranges, and colorful candy, hang our fanciful cookies called*
> Theeletterchen und den Weihnachtsbaum *[Christmas Tree Cookies].*
> *Some are made from reproductions of the original 1849 cookie cutters.*

The cookies, or "delicate tea cakes for the Christmas tree," they make each year for their tree come from their great-grandmother's 1840 recipe.

"In my childhood, on a ranch altogether out of reach of bookstores and libraries, Christmas was always a time of oranges and new books. The oranges went fast. Some of the books will be in my house and in me when I die."

"Books and Christmas"
by J. Frank Dobie
Southwest Review, winter 1951

Theeletterchen und den Weihnachtsbaum
Christmas Tree Cookies

4 cups sifted flour
1 cup butter
3½ cups granulated sugar

3 eggs
1 tsp. lemon extract
½ tsp. almond extract

Combine the flour and butter. Cut in butter with pastry blender until mixture resembles coarse meal. Add sugar and mix well. Add eggs one at a time, mixing well after each addition. Add extracts; mix. Knead dough on lightly floured surface until smooth. Place dough in plastic bag; seal and store in refrigerator until day of baking.

Bring dough to room temperature. Roll out the dough to ¼-inch thickness and cut into shapes with cookie cutters. Pierce each cookie with a sharp tool to make a hole so that it can be hung on the tree. The leftover dough can be rolled to make little sausages. Embed string lengthwise in the little sausages so that they can be strung together. Bake on low heat, 300° F for 12 to 15 minutes. Do not let the cookies brown, so that the decorating and coloring will show.

DECORATING THE COOKIES

Mix together egg white and food coloring to obtain the desired colors. For white color, mix 1 tablespoon flour with 1 cup powdered sugar and enough water to make a sticky paint. (This can also be used to stick cotton to the cookies.) When painting the cookies, do not let the different colors touch. You can glue on colored beads with plain egg white.

(FROM As We Remember . . . Bread Pudding & Wine Sauce)
used by permission from Sunrise Rotary Scholarship Foundation

As a Texas tradition, Christmas Eve has always included family favorites of Chili, Tortilla Soup, Tamales, and of course corn bread. After we relocated to Fredericksburg and created COOKING WITH FRIENDS, *an in-house cooking school featuring guest chefs, many of the German traditions and recipes have made their way into our kitchen. Instead of our usual corn bread, we have now incorporated this old German recipe, which has easily become a family favorite, into our holiday menu.*

POLENTA SQUARES

1 cup yellow cornmeal	2 ¾ cups boiling water
1 cup milk	8 oz. pork sausage
1 tsp. sugar	½ Tbsp. butter
1 tsp. salt	Maple syrup (optional)

Cook, crumble, and drain sausage; set aside. In saucepan, combine cornmeal, milk, sugar, and salt; gradually stir in water. Cook and stir until thickened and bubbly. Reduce heat; cook, covered, for 10 minutes longer or until very thick, stirring occasionally.

Remove from heat and stir in sausage. Pour into greased 7½" x 3½" x 2" loaf pan. Cover with plastic wrap and refrigerate. To serve, unmold and cut into slices. Dip both sides in flour. Melt butter in skillet over medium heat; brown slices on both sides. Serve with maple syrup, if desired.

—**JAN B. BAILEY,** *owner & chef*
COOKING WITH FRIENDS in Fredericksburg

LEMON VERBENA SUGAR COOKIES

½ cup sugar	2 cups plus 2 Tbsp.
½ cup powdered sugar	unbleached all-purpose flour
1 6-inch sprig fresh lemon verbena, about 10 leaves	½ tsp. baking soda
	½ tsp. cream of tartar
OR grated zest from 1 lemon	½ tsp. lemon extract
1 cup unsalted butter, softened	¼ tsp. salt
1 large egg	sugar for garnish

Preheat oven to 375° F. In a mini-food processor, combine the sugars and lemon verbena leaves (or lemon zest). In a medium bowl, cream together the butter with the sugar mixture. Add egg. Thoroughly blend flour, baking soda, cream of tartar, lemon extract, and salt into creamed butter. Shape dough into 6 to 12 large balls. Place 3 to 4 inches apart on lightly greased cookie sheets. Using a small, flat-bottomed glass, flatten each ball to about ¼ inch thick, dipping glass in sugar each time. If desired, garnish cookies with an additional sprinkle of sugar. Bake about 18 to 22 minutes, or until edges are lightly browned. Transfer cookies to rack to cool. 6 to 12 servings.

Lemon verbena is considered the queen of aromatic herbs. No one knows this better than the Germans who immigrated to Texas with a heritage of flavorful cooking. Herb-loving cooks continue to add lemon verbena to baked sweets, hot teas, and cooling beverages.

Everyone looks forward to nibbling these simple cookies with Gluhwein!

—**SYLVIA AND WILLIAM VARNEY,**
Proprietors, Fredericksburg Herb Farm

GLUHWEIN

1 fifth red, white, or rose wine	¼ tsp. cloves
½ cup sugar	⅛ tsp. nutmeg
¼ tsp. cinnamon	Garnish with thin orange slices,
¼ tsp. allspice	rosemary sprigs

Combine all ingredients except wine in 2-quart saucepan. Heat slowly, until sugar is dissolved. Stir in wine and continue heating until mixture is just below boiling point. Strain into 6 heated mugs. Garnish with a thin slice of orange and a small sprig of rosemary, if desired. 6 servings.

Fredericksburg "old-timers" say that early settlers concocted this warmer-upper as a remedy for the bleakness of their winter Hill Country community. Most worked long hours outdoors, even up to Christmas Eve, regardless of how chilly or gray. Once home, they would pour wine into a crock and add some sweetening ingredients, then thrust a red-hot poker into the mixture—just as their Bavarian fathers had done. The poker, in addition to heating the wine, made it luminous. Thus, the name "Gluhwein," or literally, "glowing wine."

—SYLVIA AND WILLIAM VARNEY,
Proprietors, Fredericksburg Herb Farm

CAMP DAVID GINGERBREAD

2 eggs, beaten	1 tsp. baking soda
1 cup buttermilk	1 tsp. ginger
1 lb. brown sugar	2 tsp. cinnamon
2 cups all-purpose flour	1 tsp. nutmeg
¾ cup butter	

Preheat oven to 350° F. Add eggs to buttermilk. Blend and set aside. Combine brown sugar and flour. Cut in butter. Reserve 1 cup of mixture for later use. To remainder of sugar mixture add baking soda, ginger, cinnamon, and nutmeg. Stir in buttermilk mixture just until all ingredients are moist. Pour batter into a 9 by 13-inch greased and floured metal baking pan. Sprinkle reserved cup of sugar mixture over top of batter. Bake 35 minutes.

—GWEN AND DAVID FULLBROOK, *Innkeepers*
Camp David, a traditional bed & breakfast in Fredericksburg

OPA'S COUNTRY SAUSAGE POTATO SOUFFLÉ

5 eggs	2 cups grated Monterey jack cheese
½ cup mayonnaise	½ lb. Opa's Country Sausage Links,
⅔ cup heavy cream	chopped and sautéed in butter,
⅔ cup half & half	then drained
1 tsp. Cavender's Seasonings	1 cup hash browns, sautéed with sausage
1 tsp. dried parsley	

Mix together eggs, cream, and mayo. Layer in 9-inch greased pie pan: 1 cup cheese, sausage, potatoes, and other cup of cheese. Pour egg mixture over top. Bake at 400° F for 50 minutes. Let sit for at least 30 to 45 minutes before cutting. Serves 6

—GWEN AND DAVID FULLBROOK, *Innkeepers*
Camp David, a traditional bed & breakfast in Fredericksburg

Rocking
(NATIVITY)

From *The Oxford Book of Carols*. Edited by Percy Dearmer, R. Vaughan Williams, and Martin Shaw. © 1964 Oxford University Press. Used by permission.

Translated by Percy Dearmer

Czech carol

1. Lit - tle Je - sus, sweet - ly sleep, do not stir; We will lend a coat of fur,
2. Ma - ry's lit - tle ba - by, sleep, sweet - ly sleep, Sleep in com - fort, slum - ber deep;

We will rock you, rock you, rock you, We will rock you, rock you, rock you:

See the fur to keep you warm, Snug - ly round your ti - ny form.
We will serve you all we can, Dar - ling, dar - ling lit - tle man.

"Veselé Vánoce"
(MERRY CHRISTMAS)
**from The Bujnoch Family—
Our Czech-American Heritage**
by Dorothy Bujnoch, Hallettsville

The Christmas holiday officially began on Christmas Eve, which was a day of fasting. Many family members said, "We were always told we might see 'zlata prasatko' (a golden pig) but we didn't know what that meant." (According to Czech tradition in the Old Country, children were encouraged to fast until the evening meal with the promise of seeing "zlata prasatko." Since the "golden pig" never appeared, for some it meant the Christmas star, the brightest sparkler, or some special reward for doing penance.) Christmas Eve meal consisted of pea soup and fish or oysters. Preparations for Christmas included baking strudels, apple cake, and kolaches. The Christmas tree, a cedar cut from the pasture, was decorated with popcorn, apples, and candy. Small wax candles were used as Christmas tree lights.

A bountiful tree at Thistle Hill in Fort Worth

Midnight Mass was followed by much awaited "klobasnicky" (sausage kolaches or "pigs-in-the-blanket"). The children enjoyed shooting firecrackers. Toys were scarce. Some received small wooden toys, a handkerchief, or a ball. For most families apples, oranges, and candy were the usual "treat." Family members said, "We could smell that box of delicious apples all over the house." Christmas dinner was a real feast, which included turkey and dressing and all the trimmings.

Christmas caroling was a regular event on the feast of St. Stephen, the day after Christmas. A group would walk from house to house, through pastures and across muddy creek beds, singing at the home of each neighbor and receiving a treat in return. Kolaches, fruit, and pigs-in-the-blanket were usual rewards. Often the group was joined by more carolers at each house. The Christmas caroling tradition lives on, but now we use a trailer lined with hay to carry us from house to house.

The families here eat fish on Christmas Eve because of the Catholic influence. Years ago, the Catholic families would fast on Christmas Eve and only eat one meal (without meat) in the evening. Although fasting is not required any longer, it is still a tradition to have a fish fry with the whole family on Christmas Eve.

*—*PAT CARR, *Hallettsville*

A CZECH-TEX CHRISTMAS
by Dr. Rick Barrett, Sugar Land

Vlastislava Peksa is my mother's maiden name, a uniquely beautiful name that is purely Czechoslovakian. "Vlast" means home, native, and mother country, and "slava" means fame and glory. My mother, born in Unin, Czechoslovakia, emigrated to the United States as a young girl, disembarking on Ellis Island in New York. After growing up, marrying, and raising a family, she eventually found herself in another new world—Houston, Texas.

Being raised in a family with such immediate and close ties to Czechoslovakia, my mother has been able to continue certain family traditions of her heritage. Although my Irish heritage from my father, Joe, is very rich, it is the Czechoslovakian traditions that permeate our home on the holidays. After all, Irish men don't cook!

As a Roman Catholic family, it is our tradition to attend midnight mass; then after mass, we all gather to exchange presents and have an early morning meal. This is just a small snack (complete with special Christmas cookies, of course) to hold us over; after all, it is 2 o'clock in the morning! This always seems to be a magical time, perhaps because the darkness gives one a special sensation of peace and tranquility or perhaps because the lights from the Christmas tree, decorations, and music transport us from the real world temporarily. It is a special time to open gifts and declare our love for one another as God's love is in our hearts and music is softly playing in the background.

After all the gift giving is done, and the house is strewn with presents and torn wrapping paper, exhaustion takes over, and we all go to sleep as Christmas Eve merges into Christmas Day. In just a few hours, the break of day will come dancing through the windows. Christmas for our family is a two-day event.

Part of the family tradition has, as in many cultures, focused around meals. This always has great meaning and gives solidarity to the family. There is no more special time to gather and enjoy a traditional meal than Christmas. My mother's special gift of love is a great meal that usually takes a day and a half to prepare and about ten minutes for us all to devour. After all, we have waited a whole year for this meal! Dinner usually consists of Kachna (roast duck), knedlicky (kin-ed-lick-ee—dumplings flattened and smothered with gravy), sweet-and-sour red cabbage, sweet green peas, and hot spiced or cold applesauce and homemade biscuits. The adults usually drink beer, and the children have cider. We top it all off with tea, coffee, and several varieties of cookies for dessert.

One of the most unique and special things that our family does is the sharing of an Oplatek. This paper-thin wafer is passed from person to person to break off and share. The wafer is the same as used at the mass, though it is unblessed. It can be dipped in honey and signifies the breaking of bread as Christ did.

CHRISTMAS BREAD (VANOCKA)

4 oz. butter	½ tsp. salt	5 cups flour
½ cup sugar	rind from ¼ lemon (¼ tsp.)	½ cup almonds, chopped
2 egg yolks	¾ cup milk, warm	½ cup raisins
1 egg	1 tsp. vanilla	beaten egg for top

Yeast sponge: Dissolve 2 packages active dry yeast in ¼ cup warm milk. Add pinch of flour and a pinch of sugar. Let stand for 10 minutes till bubbly.

Cream butter with sugar and egg yolks, egg, lemon rind, salt, and vanilla. Add yeast mixture to creamed ingredients; then, alternately add flour and milk. Knead to stiff dough, add chopped nuts and raisins and lemon juice to taste. Cover bowl with cloth and let rise for 1 hour in a warm place. Divide risen dough into 9 similar pieces and roll each piece into a 12-inch rope. Braid first 4 together; put on greased pan, sealing together at one end. Brush with beaten egg. Then braid 3 more pieces together and put them on top of the braided 4 pieces and brush with egg. Last, take 2 pieces of dough and twist these around each other and put on top of the 3 pieces. Brush again and let rise. Brush again and first bake at 400° F. When it has risen in oven and just started to turn color, turn temperature to 325° F and finish baking, about 50–60 minutes altogether.

Note: If you like to have chopped nuts on top, then spread them on bread before putting it in oven.

—**ANNE RHODES**, *Hallettsville*

ROAST DUCK (KACHNA)

1 duck, 5 lbs. or more
salt, pepper, paprika, caraway seeds
¼ onion and/or apple

Clean and wash duck inside and out. Pat dry; rub cavity with salt, pepper, and paprika; sprinkle in some caraway seeds. Insert ¼ piece of onion and/or apple. Rub outside of duck with salt, pepper, and paprika. Sprinkle with caraway seeds. Place duck in shallow roasting pan with small amount of water. Roast in preheated 325° F oven for 2–2½ hours. After about ¾ of an hour take duck out and, with a fork, prick the skin around the joints and any other fatty area to release the grease. Do this a few times until no more grease comes to the surface. Drain any grease into a pot or bowl and add about ¼ inch of water to the drippings in the pan; this will make a nice brown gravy. When duck is cooked, remove from pan, make gravy, and ENJOY! (Discard onion and/or apple.)

To make gravy, add more water and scrape drippings in pan. Estimate liquid left in pan and use approximately 1 Tbsp. flour to a cup of the liquid in pan. Stir until it thickens.

—**VLASTA BARRETT**, *Missouri City*

Military reenactments bring history vividly to light

Christmas at Old Fort Concho

SAN ANGELO, FIRST WEEKEND IN DECEMBER

Our family loves Christmas at Old Fort Concho—three days filled with all types of crafts and shows by Fort Concho soldiers.

—MARY LOU FULLER,
San Angelo

Regimental colors unfurl in the brisk West Texas wind as the Memorial 16th Regiment, U.S. Infantry, sets up camp on Fort Concho's quadrangle parade ground. Costumed fur trappers, sutlers, scouts, Native Americans, and traders bustle around the grounds building campfires and unloading wagons. Merchants and artisans set up their booths and display their wares. Volunteers light luminarias and lamps in and around the twenty restored historic buildings, each decorated to represent a different Christmas or ethnic era. At last, the *biggest* and the *best* annual frontier Christmas event in Texas is ready to welcome its 40,000 visitors to experience a rootin'-tootin', Fort Concho–style, holiday extravaganza!

Fort Concho, established in 1867 along the banks of the Concho River as a cavalry and infantry outpost, saw active service for more than two turbulent decades during the settling of the vast West Texas frontier. Now, as *Christmas at Old Fort Concho* visitors stroll through this National Historic Landmark's native limestone buildings or witness historic re-creations on the quadrangle, they can experience anew that bygone era when times were hard and soldiers were far from home.

Golden stars and a patchwork quilt invoke Christmases past

From the first blast of reveille to the last note of retreat, Fort Concho comes alive with the sights and sounds of days gone by. The sound of hoofbeats, shouts of drill sergeants, and cannon fire bring the sound of the past to the present. Campfires entice you with the aroma of strong coffee, and perhaps there's a dutch oven of biscuits or stew. However, it's not ALL work and no play, as the cowboys will pick and sing, or just relate the trials of frontier life.

—LINDA HERMES, *Fort Concho volunteer*

Since frontier winters in the 1870s and 1880s were bleak times filled with unrest and fear, Christmas celebrations were eagerly anticipated events. Soldiers and families at Fort Concho planned special meals and held elaborate parties and dances, using any available trees and decorations to produce a festive atmosphere. Soldiers especially loved planning special surprise presents for the few children at the fort. In 1875, one such soldier gave Colonel Grierson's son, George, a little brown puppy—much to the delight of both George and the puppy! Instead of the modern custom of putting wrapped toys under the tree for the children, the tradition at Fort Concho was to hang the toys in amongst the branches of the huge tree in Officer's Quarters No. 1 (exceptions being made for the puppy variety, of course). Whatever the activity, Christmas became a time of renewal and hope—a treasured time of togetherness.

Four days after Christmas in 1845, the U.S. Congress accepted the Texas state constitution, thus giving Texas the gift of statehood as a belated Christmas present.

And togetherness is what *Christmas at Old Fort Concho* is all about. Every year, the first weekend in December is jam-packed with nonstop activity and entertainment for "kids" of all ages. One perennial visitor to the event reports, "It isn't just the cowboy events, or the children's arts and crafts activities, or the shopping, or the food (well, maybe it is the German sausage and the warm funnel cakes!). It isn't even the living history reenactments that make this weekend so special. It's the almost overwhelming feeling of connection to everyone who ever lived and loved or fought and died on this wild frontier. That's what brings our family back every year to start our Christmas holidays here at Fort Concho."

A "living history" Christmas reenactment in Goliad

"Christmas Along the Corridor"

Christmas Creek, which rises in Limestone County, received its name in 1855 when surveyors camped there on Christmas Day.

During the first weekend of December, the air is filled with excitement as communities all along the historic 90-mile Alamo-La Bahia corridor eagerly await the arrival of the Official Pony Express Christmas Couriers as part of their weekend of holiday festivities. The Couriers, who have been specially sworn in for this event, depart about 8:00 A.M. from Presidio La Bahia, where the festivities for the Texas Frontier Rendezvous, a living history encampment depicting pre-1840s frontier days, are just getting started. The riders gallop to Goliad's courthouse square for a reading of the Governor's Proclamation, and then they are off to San Antonio along three simultaneous routes, carrying the Proclamation and season's greetings to each town and changing riders and horses until they all converge at Fort Sam Houston around 4:30 P.M. for the grand finale. Special Pony Express stamp cancellations, which are available at the temporary postal stations in each of the corridor towns, add that nostalgic Old West touch that Christmas card recipients all over the country enjoy.

A Pony Express courier ready to ride

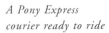

Fulton Mansion State Historical Park
ROCKPORT/FULTON

Along the Gulf coast, Fulton Mansion, a magnificent French Second Empire–style house built in 1877, takes on a holiday luster as softly glowing luminarias line the pathways in preparation for the annual "Christmas at the Mansion" celebration. A recent theme, "A Cowboy Christmas," came alive as the Badland Rangers, a living history organization, reenacted life on the range a hundred years ago. Outside the mansion, cowboys relaxed around a smoldering campfire and demonstrated their gun handling prowess. Inside, costumed ladies practiced old-fashioned handwork techniques to the delight and amazement of the visitors.

Horse-drawn carriage rides, always a popular part of the celebration, give visitors a nostalgic flavor of simpler times as they tour the luminaria-lit park. Another special treat is the long-robed Father Christmas who strides around the grounds carrying his bag of toys and checking in with wide-eyed youngsters to see if they've been good this year.

From the living history reenactments to Father Christmas to horse-drawn carriage rides, "Christmas at the Mansion" wraps hours of fun, history, and Victorian holiday splendor into one big "package" for the whole family.

*Father Christmas
lends a willing ear*

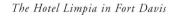

The Hotel Limpia in Fort Davis

Hotel Limpia
FORT DAVIS

Built in 1912, twenty-one years after the army closed nearby Fort Davis, Hotel Limpia quickly attracted tourists escaping the summer heat in the cool Davis Mountains. The hotel, built of local pink limestone, offered elegant pressed-tin ceilings with rounded corners, gaslights and turn-of-the-century oak furniture—luxurious surroundings compared with the Old Fort buildings that had previously been the only accommodations available in the area.

The Limpia flourished for many years, even adding an annex in 1920; but as so often happens, changes in the hotel and changes in the times caused a decline. The building housed a series of offices and businesses over the years until 1972, when J. C. Duncan, teacher and superintendent of schools, bought the building and used it as a government class project. He had his classes make models of the historic town square as it was in the early 1900s. This later led to a full restoration of the hotel spurred on by the enthusiasm of the students.

Now Hotel Limpia, restored and remodeled, continues its West Texas tradition of offering a relaxing place to "hang a hat" while enjoying a holiday mountain retreat, touring Fort Davis, or trekking to the stars via McDonald Observatory, which is 17 miles up the canyon.

Collin Street Bakery
CORSICANA

What do Ringling Brothers, Barnum & Bailey Circus performers have in common with Vanna White, Zubin Mehta, and executives of the European Space Agency? They are just a few on the list of fruitcake connoisseurs from every state and 196 nations around the world who agree that it just wouldn't be Christmas without a DeLuxe Fruitcake from Corsicana's Collin Street Bakery.

This extraordinary fruitcake had its humble beginnings in 1896, when German baker Gus Weidmann and his partner, Tom McElwee, opened the original Collin Street Bakery and began making the cakes to market locally. By 1906, with Tom McElwee's expanding marketing efforts and the fruitcake's growing list of devotees in every major city, Tom and Gus were able to build an enormous new bakery and a fancy private hotel. Through these doors came hundreds of celebrated visitors from all walks of life—and Tom made sure each one had an extra cake in his trunk as he or she boarded the outbound train!

In 1913, the bakery's mail-order business escalated dramatically when Ringling Brothers Circus performers were so taken with the local fruitcake that they ordered cakes to be sent to friends all around the country. Now, Collin Street Bakery sends out over a million DeLuxe Fruitcakes annually—every one decorated by hand the old-fashioned way, using enormous native Texas pecans. It's no wonder Corsicana calls itself "The Fruitcake Capitol of the World!"

Above: The celebrated fruitcake of Corsicana's Collin Street Bakery
Overleaf: Palo Duro Canyon State Park, dusty with the season's first snowfall

"Dear Santa, I hope you enjoy your milk and cookies Texas-style."

CHRISTMAS MEMORIES

by Ann Mason, Liberty Hills

The excitement of Christmas began in our home in rural Cherokee County when Mama decided to bake the fruitcake. She had all nine of us kids cracking hickory and black walnuts around the fireplace hearth, using the flatiron to crack the shells. Daddy was always having to fill in the holes on the hearth! The Christmas fruitcake was baked about six weeks before Christmas, soaked in "medicinal rum," and wrapped in a clean cloth and put in the flour barrel for safekeeping.

The whole house would be permeated by the aroma of roasting peanuts, and for weeks the nine kids would pour over the Sears catalog wishing and hoping. My younger sister and I would get a doll and set of dishes and the two younger boys cap pistols and caps or a toy car.

On Christmas morning we all received a brown paper sack with an apple, orange, nuts, and hard candy. The boys would get firecrackers in their sacks and would rise at the crack of dawn to beat the other boys to waking up the neighborhood with the sounds of fireworks going off.

I remember the last Christmas of my childhood in 1942 when Daddy was working in Galveston helping to build Camp Wallace. He brought my little sister and me two beautiful big dolls. To keep them a surprise he left them at his cousin Bill's house. Shortly after Christmas, I was admiring cousin Bill's new baby daughter, and I told him she was the prettiest thing I had ever seen, except for my doll!

The Pecan
"OFFICIAL STATE TREE OF TEXAS"
(AND UNOFFICIAL STATE RECIPE INGREDIENT!)

When asked to clarify her recipe ingredients that called for 1 cup of "nuts," one long-time Texas cook just laughed and replied, "Honey, in Texas, everybody knows that 'pecan' [pronounced puh-CAHN] and 'nut' are synonymous because there is only one nut worth puttin' in your mouth!" After tasting over thirty pecan recipes submitted for this book, our happy tasters have rated the following recipes the best of the best.

CRUSTLESS PECAN PIE

2 eggs
1 cup sugar
½ cup flour
1 ½ sticks oleo, melted
1 ⅓ cups angel flake coconut
1 cup pecans, chopped
1 tsp. vanilla

Whip eggs together. Add sugar and flour and whip together well. Add rest of ingredients and mix well. Put mixture in buttered and floured 9" glass pie pan.

Bake at 325° F for 25–30 minutes.

—**DOROTHY PECHAL**, *Temple Museum Curator, SPJST*

We've used this Pecan Tassies recipe in our family for years, and everyone loves them. (They look like little pecan pies!)

—**MELINDA KURZ**

PECAN TASSIES

½ cup butter or margarine, softened
1 package cream cheese (3 oz.), softened
1 cup all-purpose flour
1 egg
¾ cup packed brown sugar
1 Tbsp. butter or margarine, softened
1 tsp. vanilla
dash salt
½ cup coarsely chopped pecans

Pastry dough: Cream together the ½ cup butter and the cream cheese. Stir in flour; mix well. Cover; chill about 1 hour.

Egg Mixture: Stir together egg, sugar, 1 Tbsp. butter, vanilla, and a dash salt just until smooth; set aside.

Shape pastry dough into two dozen 1-inch balls; place each in ungreased 1 ¾-inch muffin cup. Press dough onto bottom and sides. Spoon about 1 teaspoon of chopped pecans into each muffin cup; fill with egg mixture.

Bake in 325° F oven about 25 minutes or until set. Cool; remove from pans.

Makes 24.

These tassies are to die for!

—**JUDITH FARROW**, *Houston*

—**MELINDA KURZ**, *Sugar Land*

Favorite Texas Pecan recipes, like Pecan Tassies, Fudge Pecan Pie, and Pecan Macaroons, delight Lone Star State party-goers

On Christmas Day, our family fries catfish, shrimp, French fries, and hush puppies served with many salads and veggies, and topped off with our favorite Pecan Pie Supreme— of course!

—CLARICE HANSTROM

I am married 56 years, and this is handed down from an aunt about 30 years ago. I make it every year for the Christmas holidays and never have any left over after the holidays.

—MILDRED O. JENSCHKE

A co-worker gave me this recipe in 1945, and I still think it is the BEST pecan pie in Texas. I suspect my method of glazing the pecans with oleo is the secret that makes my pie everybody's favorite. One tip I'd like to pass on is that anytime you bake a pie in an aluminum pan (like the unbaked pastry shells come in), make sure you put the pie on an aluminum cookie pan so the bottom of the crust will brown as well.

—MARY BUEHRING

PECAN PIE SUPREME

3 eggs
½ cup sugar
1 cup corn syrup (I use part maple syrup)
⅛ tsp. salt

1 tsp. vanilla
¼ cup butter or margarine
1 cup pecans
1 unbaked pastry shell

Place the pecans in the bottom of an unbaked pastry shell. Mix the other ingredients in order and pour over pecans.

Bake at 350° F for 50–60 minutes. The pecans will rise to the top and form a crusted layer.

—CLARICE HANSTROM, *Hutto*

HOLIDAY LEMON-PECAN FRUITCAKE

1 lb. box brown sugar
1 lb. butter, softened
6 eggs, separated; set whites aside
2 cups flour
1 tsp. baking powder
½ tsp. salt
1 oz. bottle lemon extract

1 quart chopped pecan halves
2 cups candied dates, chopped
½ lb. candied pineapple, chopped
¼ lb. candied red cherries
¼ lb. candied green cherries
2 cups flour

Separate eggs, reserving egg whites for later use. Cream together sugar and butter; add beaten egg yolks and mix well. Combine 2 cups flour, baking powder, and salt; add to creamed mixture. Add lemon extract.

Coat pecans, dates, and fruit with 2 cups flour; mix well and add to creamed mixture. Beat egg whites until stiff, then fold into batter. Cover and let stand overnight.

Next day, press mixture into greased and floured tube pan, or 2 loaf pans. Bake at 275° F for 1½ hours for small pans, or 2 to 2½ hours for large pan. If it gets too brown, place a small sheet of foil on top. Can be made ahead and frozen.

—MILDRED O. JENSCHKE, *Stonewall*

PECAN PIE

3 eggs
1 cup sugar
1 cup blue label Karo
¼ tsp. salt

2 tsp. vanilla
1½ cups chopped pecans
½ stick oleo, melted

Beat eggs, then add sugar, Karo, salt, vanilla, and half of oleo. Stir well. Stir in pecans. Pour into unbaked pie shell. Use back of spoon to spread the remaining oleo over top of pie mixture—this gives the pecans a kind of glaze as well as a toasted flavor. Bake at 350° F for 45 minutes. Cool on rack.

—MARY BUEHRING, *Sugar Land*

MAMA LOU'S BANANA NUT CAKE

1 cup oleo	4 eggs
6 bananas	3 cups flour
8 Tbsp. buttermilk	2 cups pecans
2 tsp. vanilla	3 cups sugar
1 tsp. baking soda	¼ tsp. salt

Use small, very ripe bananas. Use small or medium eggs. Cream sugar and butter until light. Add eggs and mix well. Cut bananas into pieces and add to mixture. Again, mix well. Sift dry ingredients together and add alternately with the buttermilk. Add vanilla and nuts. Mix until blended. Pour into a well-greased and floured large tube pan. (I use Baker's Joy to do this.)

Bake 1 hour in oven preheated to 350° F.

Mama Lou checked to see if it was done inside by using a broom straw. Perhaps today, we would prefer a small skewer (a toothpick may not be long enough). Be sure to check close to center since that's the part that tends to need more time. Cool for a while in the pan, which is inverted on a rack. Remove cake from pan and serve it "right side up." Enjoy!

— **JANE CLANCY DEBENPORT,** *Temple*

A gingerbread village crafted by The Gingerbread Architects (Dan and Mickey Hillsman, Loraine Zaiontz, and Elaine Marshall)

FUDGE PECAN PIE

1 stick of margarine	⅛ tsp. salt
2 cups hot water	2 tsps. vanilla
7 Tbsp. cocoa	1 large can evaporated milk
4 cups sugar	1 cup chopped pecans
1 cup flour	2 10" pie shells, unbaked

Melt margarine in hot water, add cocoa and let dissolve. Then add rest of ingredients. Pour ½ of amount into each pie shell. Bake at 350° F until brown—approximately 1 hour.

— **KAREN SKRIVANEK,** *Sealy*

BUTTERMILK PRALINES

2 cups sugar	2 Tbsp. butter or margarine
1 cup buttermilk	1 tsp. vanilla
1 tsp. baking soda	2 cups pecans, coarsely broken
2 Tbsp. light corn syrup	

Combine sugar, buttermilk, baking soda, and corn syrup in large saucepan. Cook over medium heat to soft-ball stage. Watch and stir often. Mixture will begin to brown. Remove from heat and add butter, vanilla, and pecans. Stir and cool until mixture thickens and takes on a slightly creamy tinge. Drop on waxed paper. When cool, you may wrap in plastic wrap or store, unwrapped, in airtight container. Makes 20 to 30.

— **SYLVIA BONIN,** *Corsicana*

Lula Ratcliff Clancy Heneghan Minter's Christmas Banana Nut Cake is now reaching down to the fifth generation. Mama Lou gave the recipe to her son's new wife (my mother). When I married, she gave it to me (her granddaughter). Mama Lou lived to the age of ninety-six years—long enough to see her great-granddaughter marry and feed the cake to HER children.

This makes a HUGE tube cake. When Mama Lou first made the cake, bananas were smaller and more expensive. Eggs were smaller and less expensive. Pecans came from her sister's tree. Butter and buttermilk were a part of any farm kitchen's ample stores. Today the fifth generation of her descendants is getting old enough to look forward to the sweet, buttery, nutty goodness of Mama Lou's Banana Nut Cake.

— **JANE CLANCY DEBENPORT**

Sometimes I make this without raisins. I just add a few more pecans or candied fruit.

—MILDRED HUDDLESTON

This is an old recipe that came from our paternal grandmother, Marie Klein Streuer. She used toast made from homemade cracked wheat bread.

—MARIE OFFERMAN

Our family used to bake sugar cookies each December using holiday cookie cutters to shape them. Once they were done, it was time to decorate! Our kitchen table would be covered with bowls of colored frosting, sprinkles, dots (my dad's favorite topping), candy, and other delights. Our whole family would use these to decorate the cookies. No two cookies ended up alike! When my sister and I were little, our cookies would be so well "decorated" that they were too sweet to eat!

—JENNIFER LATHAM,
Lewisville

WHISKEY LIZZIES

½ cup butter	1 tsp. nutmeg
1 cup brown sugar	1 tsp. cinnamon
4 eggs	1 tsp. cloves
3 Tbsp. sweet milk	6 cups pecans
2⅔ tsp. soda	1 lb. white raisins
3 cups sifted flour	1 lb. candied red cherries
⅔ cup whiskey	½ lb. candied pineapple

Cream butter and sugar thoroughly; add eggs one at a time, beating well after each addition. Alternately add liquids with sifted dry ingredients—beginning and ending with flour.

Sift ½ cup flour over raisins, pecans, cherries and pineapple. Mix into dough. Drop by teaspoonful on greased cookie sheets. Bake in 300° F oven for 30 minutes.

—MILDRED HUDDLESTON

PECAN MACAROONS

1 lb. coarsely chopped pecans	¼ tsp. cinnamon
1 lb. powdered sugar, sifted	2 pieces dry toast,
4 egg whites	ground to make fine crumbs

Beat the egg whites until stiff (the consistency of thick whipped cream). Gradually add the sugar and cinnamon. Fold in bread crumbs, then pecans. Drop by rounded teaspoonfuls onto greased cookie sheets. Bake at 300° F for 15 to 25 minutes, depending on the size of cookie. Remove from pan immediately, cool on rack.

Makes 3 to 4 dozen, depending on size. Store in a tightly sealed container.

—MARIE OFFERMAN
(from HOLIDAY REFLECTIONS COOK BOOK)
used by permission from Sophienburg Museum and Archives—New Braunfels

Another creation of The Gingerbread Architects

MEMORIES OF CHRISTMAS IN THE WHITE HOUSE
by *Lady Bird Johnson*

The Christmas season is a magical time in the White House! Christmas for the Johnsons always has meant the LBJ Ranch, but during our time when Lyndon was president, we spent two wonderful Christmases at the White House.

The first, in 1967, we gathered in our favorite yellow oval room on the second floor to open presents around the tree. All eyes were on our darling grandson, Lyn (Nugent), and on our two sons-in-law who soon were to leave for service in the Marines and Air Force. Like some lovely, fragile bubble, it was a moment to catch and hold and remember.

Firelight danced on the Christmas tree star, the same star that had been used by the Roosevelts when they lived in the White House. Stockings hung from the mantel with symbolic decorations that told an amusing story of each of our lives (those same stockings have increased in number over the years and are still hung with loving care). Everyone waited with bated breath for their own gifts to be opened. I was anxious to see if Lynda was as pleased with her original edition of Dickens as I hoped she would be and whether Luci liked the "Little Boy" suits selected for Lyn as much as we did. And from the ranch, we distributed gifts of jellies and preserves and corn relishes and pickled okra and pears—a beautiful bounty transported north! Lyndon's gifts were the most generous and most glamorous that year and every year—he always was one of Santa's best helpers!

Christmas of 1968 was a particular time of joy for us. There was a special feeling of closeness to family and friends and reflections on jobs done with heart and hope, along with expectations about the time to come. We were looking forward to going home to the ranch with its fields of wildflowers to renew us—and for Lyndon to start afresh. He eagerly looked forward to helping young people prepare for their future. That Christmas, our last in the White House and in Washington, was a glorious chapter in our lives that was drawing to a close. So many changes had been wrought in our lives while we lived in that house. Truly, we counted our blessings.

LBJ RANCH PICKLED OKRA

3 lb. whole okra
6 hot peppers
6 cloves peeled garlic
1 quart vinegar
1 ⅓ cups water
½ cup salt
1 Tbsp. mustard seed

Wash okra and pack in clean jars. Add to each jar 1 hot pepper and 1 clove of garlic.

Bring remaining ingredients to a boil. Cover okra with hot liquid, filling to within ½ inch of jar top. Adjust lids. Process in boiling water for 10 minutes.

CHEESE WAFERS

1 cup margarine or soft butter
2 cups flour
8 oz. sharp cheddar cheese, grated
1 tsp. cayenne pepper
½ tsp. salt
2 cups Rice Krispies cereal

Cut butter into flour; add cheese and seasonings. Fold in cereal. Drop by small rounds on an ungreased cookie sheet and flatten with a spoon. *Bake* at 350 °F for about 15 minutes (careful not to get too brown).

LACE COOKIES

½ cup flour
½ cup coconut
¼ cup Karo syrup (red or blue label)
¼ cup brown sugar, firmly packed
¼ cup margarine
½ tsp. vanilla

Mix flour with coconut. Mix Karo syrup, sugar, and margarine until well blended. Cook over medium heat, stirring constantly. Remove from heat and stir in vanilla. Gradually blend in flour mixture.

Drop by teaspoonfuls 3 to 4 inches apart on ungreased cookie sheet. Bake at 325° F for 5–7 minutes. Let cool one minute, then remove quickly to wire racks to finish cooling.

My mom's family grew up near Burnet and Lampasas. In that part of Texas, holly and ivy were scarce. Thorn bushes, however, grew abundantly. As Christmas neared, my grandmother would send one of the boys out to cut a limb from one of the thorn bushes. They would impale it on a nail stuck through a small board. The whole thing was then painted white and studded with "snow" (Lux flakes added when the paint was wet). On each thorn, Mammaw stuck a bright, fat gumdrop. The kids would pick a treat, then Mammaw would replenish the tree! What a wonderful memory.

—**JANE CLANCY DEBENPORT,**
Temple

Living in the country enabled my family to have a plentiful supply of milk, eggs, and butter. Mother, Ethel Clements Thompson, would sell enough poultry to buy sugar and flour in 100 pound sacks. Our trips to town were seldom, so 100 pounds would last a reasonable length of time.

—**ANICE THOMPSON VANCE**

MOM'S THIMBLE COOKIES

2 cups sifted flour	1 egg
1 ½ tsp. baking powder	1 egg yolk
½ tsp. salt	½ tsp. vanilla
¾ cup shortening (margarine)	3 Tbsp. milk
⅔ cup brown sugar, firmly packed	1 egg white, slightly beaten
⅓ cup Karo syrup (blue label)	2 Tbsp. water
jam or jelly	1 ½ cups nuts, finely chopped

Sift together flour, baking powder, and salt; set aside. Cream shortening; add sugar. Beat until fluffy. Add Karo syrup and blend. Add egg and egg yolk, beating thoroughly after each addition. Stir in vanilla. Add sifted dry ingredients alternately with milk. Mix thoroughly. Chill dough. (Dough will be very sticky.)

Roll chilled dough into 1-inch balls and dip in slightly beaten egg white and water mix. Roll in chopped nuts. Place 1 inch apart on ungreased baking sheet. Bake at 375° F for 5 minutes. Remove from oven and make a depression on each cookie with thumb or spoon. Fill each depression with jam or jelly and return to oven and bake about 10 minutes longer.

—**DOTTIE PRIGER,** *Houston*

MAMA'S APPLESAUCE CAKE

½ cup shortening (Crisco)	1 tsp. cloves
1 cup sugar	1 tsp. allspice
1 cup apples, cooked, mashed, and cooled (about 4 small apples)	1 tsp. nutmeg
	1 cup nuts, chopped
2 cups flour	1 jar mincemeat
1 tsp. cinnamon	1 tsp. soda, dissolved in 1 tsp. hot water

Mix shortening and sugar, then put in cool applesauce, flour, spices, nuts, and mincemeat. Then add soda. Beat and put in long pan (9" by 13") or muffin tins. Bake for 30 minutes at 350° F.

—**EMMA GENE SCHROEDER,** *Wharton*

MOTHER'S BUTTER CAKE

1 cup butter (real butter!)	1 ½ cups all-purpose flour
1 cup eggs (usually 5 small or 4 large)	1 tsp. vanilla
1 ½ cups sugar	

Cream butter and sugar. Add unbeaten eggs; add vanilla; add flour and mix well until sugar is dissolved. Bake in loaf pan about 1 hour at 350° F.

—**ANICE THOMPSON VANCE,** *Temple*

PUMPKIN ROLL

1½ cups white sugar	2 tsp. soda	⅔ cup water
1½ cups brown sugar	1½ tsp. salt	1 tsp. vanilla
1 can pumpkin (2 cups)	1½ tsp. cinnamon	1 cup chopped pecans
4 eggs	1 tsp. nutmeg	1 cup Angel Flake coconut
1 cup oil or shortening	3½ cups flour	

Beat eggs, sugar, oil, and pumpkin until well blended. Add dry ingredients and water and vanilla—stir until well blended. Spray 4 one-pound coffee cans with nonstick spray and put equal amounts of batter in each of them. Bake at 350° F for 1 hour.

—LOIS GAINER, *Hutto*

We bake forty or fifty of these "coffee can cakes" each Christmas, then wrap them in foil and freeze them. They make great gifts for our drop-in friends or church friends.

—LOIS GAINER

DEEP, DARK CHOCOLATE CAKE

2 cups sugar	1½ tsp. baking powder	1 cup milk
1¾ cups flour	1½ tsp. baking soda	½ cup vegetable oil
¾ cup Hershey's European-style Cocoa	1 tsp. salt	2 tsp. vanilla
	2 eggs	1 cup boiling water

Spray two 9-inch round pans or one 9" by 13" pan with Pam. (I line round pans with wax paper, too, for ease in removal.) Preheat oven to 350° F.

Mix sugar, flour, cocoa, baking powder, baking soda, and salt. Add eggs, milk, oil, and vanilla. Beat 2 minutes. Stir in 1 cup boiling water. Batter will be thin. Pour into prepared pans.

Bake at 350° F for 30–35 minutes for round pans; 35–40 minutes for 9" by 13" pan.

Cool in pans 10 minutes. Remove and finish cooling on wire rack.

WHITE CHOCOLATE BUTTER CREAM FROSTING

Bring cream to boil; pour over chocolate and stir until smooth. Stir in crème de cacao and cool, stirring occasionally. Set aside.

Cream butter; add powdered sugar and beat for 5 minutes until light and fluffy.

6 Tbsp. heavy cream	2 sticks unsalted butter
4 oz. white chocolate, chopped	4 cups powdered sugar
¼ cup crème de cacao	

Add white chocolate mixture gradually, beating until right consistency.

—LANNA KUEHL, *Houston*

Mammaw tried valiantly to make cookies for the grand kids at Christmas. Her recipe called for the dough to be wrapped in a damp towel and chilled. Her problem: the kids preferred the dough to the cookies. By the time she took the towel out of the refrigerator, there was rarely enough to cook, and we were too full to care!

—JANE CLANCY DEBENPORT, *Temple*

This cake is moist and rich. I like to frost it with "White Chocolate Butter Cream Frosting," but it is great with any frosting.

—LANNA KUEHL

Christmas Cards Along the Highway (Hwy 90), Hondo

47

CHOCOLATE RUM CAKE

1 Duncan Hines devil's food cake mix	4 eggs
1 4 oz. (small box) vanilla instant pudding	6 oz. chocolate chips
½ cup of light rum	3 oz. coconut
½ cup water	½ cup pecans, chopped
½ cup vegetable oil	

Grease bundt pan and put ½ cup pecans in the pan. Blend first six ingredients and mix at medium speed for 2 minutes. After mixing, stir in chocolate chips and coconut. Pour ingredients into pan with pecans and bake 1 hour at 325° F.

Just before cake is done, make a glaze by boiling for 2 minutes:

1 stick of real butter	¼ cup of light rum
1 cup sugar	¼ cup of water

Remove cake from oven and spoon hot glaze over the cake while still in the pan. Let cake absorb the glaze 45 to 60 minutes before turning out on a plate.

—**CLAUDINE AYRES,** *Sealy*

STRUDEL

Dough for four strudels:	*Filling for each strudel use:*
2 egg yolks	4 cups thinly sliced or shredded apples
1 cup milk	1 cup crumbs (crushed vanilla wafers,
3 cups flour	graham crackers, saltines, or crumbled
6 Tbsp. oleo or butter	bread—or mixture of these)
⅛ tsp. salt	1 cup sugar, with cinnamon to taste
	¼ cup coconut
	¼ cup raisins
	¼ cup chopped pecans
	melted butter or margarine, as desired

The strudel is baked about three times a year in Hallettsville by the Sacred Heart School and the American Cancer Society as a fund-raiser and is made with local pears or Hill Country apples, depending on the time of year. It is an art that is passed down from mother to daughter.

—**VERNEL BOZKA**

Measure flour and salt in bowl. Work in softened oleo until crumbly. Beat eggs and milk and add to mixture. Mix together. Knead dough until smooth. If sticky, add more flour, being careful not to add too much. Divide dough into four balls, approximately 7 ½ to 8 oz. each. Wrap each in foil or plastic wrap. Put in covered container. Let stand at room temperature for several hours or overnight. On a floured cloth, roll out one ball of dough in a circle, approximately 18–20 inches in diameter. Brush with butter. Spread evenly over dough the apples, crumbs, sugar/cinnamon mix, coconut, raisins, and pecans. Drizzle generously with melted butter or margarine. Take end of towel and roll the dough up similar to a jelly roll, but slightly pressed down. Seal ends and brush top with melted butter. Place on greased cookie sheet. Bake in a 350° F oven for 50–60 minutes or until golden brown. After removing from oven, brush with melted butter and sprinkle with mixture of sugar and cinnamon.

If desired, raw strudel may be wrapped in aluminum foil and frozen to bake weeks or months later. When preparing a frozen strudel, put strudel directly from the freezer into the oven on a baking sheet; do not thaw. Unwrap foil; turn down at sides. Bake at 275° F for 30 minutes. Turn oven up to 350° F and continue baking for an additional 50–60 minutes or until golden brown.

—**VERNEL BOZKA,** *Hallettsville*

BANANA STRUDEL CAKE

2 cups flour

1½ cups sugar

1 tsp. baking soda

2 eggs, beaten

½ cup oil (any kind)

⅓ cup buttermilk

2 tsp. vanilla

3 ripe bananas, mashed

½ cup chopped coconut

½ cup light brown sugar

½ cup chopped pecans

Sift together flour, sugar, and baking soda. Add eggs, oil, buttermilk, and vanilla. Mix thoroughly. Add bananas and beat well. Pour batter into greased and floured 13" by 9" Pyrex cake pan.

Mix together coconut, brown sugar, and pecans for topping. Put on top of raw cake batter and bake at 350° F for 25 to 30 minutes.

—**GLADYS KERSTEN,** *Sealy*

ROYAL COCOA CHIFFON CAKE

¾ cup boiling water

½ cup cocoa

1¾ cups sugar

1¾ cups flour

3 tsps. baking powder

½ cup oil

7 egg yolks

1 tsp. vanilla

1 tsp. almond flavoring

1 cup egg whites

½ tsp. cream of tartar

Preheat oven to 325° F.

Stir cocoa into boiling water until smooth, then cool.

Sift together sugar, flour, and baking powder. Make a well and add oil, egg yolks, and cooled cocoa mixture. Add flavorings and beat mixture until smooth.

Beat egg whites with cream of tartar until stiff, but not dry. Pour egg yolk mixture over beaten whites and gently fold together. Pour into ungreased angel food cake pan and bake at 325° F for 55 minutes. Turn oven up to 350° F and bake for an additional 3 minutes. Remove from oven and invert to cool completely.

ICING

4 cups sifted powdered sugar

2 large eggs

⅔ cups margarine

2 squares melted bitter chocolate

1 tsp. vanilla

½ tsp. almond flavoring

toasted pecan bits or slivered almonds

Beat together sugar, eggs, flavorings, and melted margarine and chocolate. Spread over cool cake and sprinkle with toasted nuts.

—**MARGUERITE STARR CRAIN,** *Midland*

I bring this festive cake every year (by popular request) to the French Onion Soup Party given by friends Christmas evening. This party is a wonderful treat, especially for those of us whose extended families live far away. We all look forward to this time of fun and fellowship each year.

—**MARGUERITE STARR CRAIN**

APPLE SPICE CAKE

1 cup butter	1 tsp. each cinnamon, nutmeg, cloves
2 cups sugar	1 cup white raisins
1 tsp. vanilla	2 cups chopped nuts
3 eggs	4 apples, peeled and diced
3 cups flour	2 tsp. baking soda

Dice apples and add soda; stir. Let stand while mixing other ingredients as follows: Cream well butter and sugar; add eggs, vanilla, and sifted dry ingredients. Then add apples, raisins, and nuts. Pour into greased and floured tube pan. Bake 1 hour (or more) at 350° F.

—MRS. O. R. BENTON, *Sealy*

SAILOR'S DUFF PUDDING

1 egg	1½ cups sifted flour
½ cup dark baking molasses	2 Tbsp. melted butter
(Brer Rabbit recommended)	1 tsp. baking soda dissolved
2 Tbsp. brown sugar	in 2 Tbsp. warm water

Mix all ingredients together; add ½ cup boiling water last. Steam mixture in a large double boiler (Dutch oven size) for one hour. Pudding will have the texture of a moist cake.

SAUCE

2 egg yolks, beaten well	2 Tbsp. cooking sherry
1 cup sugar	½ pint whipping cream

Whip cream to medium stiffness. Add eggs, sugar, and sherry to whipped cream, stirring after each addition. Chill sauce while pudding is steaming.

Cut pudding into servings like you would cut a cake or pie. Cover with two to three tablespoonfuls of sauce—the more sauce the better!

—ELLEN EARLE, *Sugar Land*

PEANUT KISSES

1¾ cups flour	½ cup peanut butter
1 tsp. baking soda	1 egg
½ tsp. salt	2 Tbsp. milk
½ cup granulated sugar	1 tsp. vanilla
½ cup brown sugar	48 milk chocolate candy kisses
½ cup shortening	

Combine all ingredients except candy kisses in large mixing bowl, and mix on low speed. Shape dough into balls, using a rounded teaspoonful for each. Roll balls in sugar; place on ungreased cookie sheets. Bake at 375° F for 10–12 minutes. Remove from oven and top each cookie immediately with a candy kiss, pressing down firmly. Makes approximately 4 dozen cookies.

—DORIS CARDIFF, *Brookshire*

An elegant, bare madrone tree in Guadalupe Mountains National Park

The first Christmas with each of my three children is a very special memory. As they've gotten older, I've caught each of them sitting in the dark under our lighted tree just staring for hours. We also like making cookies—we bake for days, and then take cookies around to those who make our lives so special.

—SUSAN WILLIAMS, *Decatur*

The Snowman tree, one of 28 decorated trees at House of the Seasons

House of the Seasons
JEFFERSON
Open for Christmas tours November 1 to January 2

Festooned with elegant lights and greenery, House of the Seasons undoubtedly fulfills the promise of its name during the Christmas season. The square cupola at the top of the house contains four walls of different-colored stained glass, each color representing a season of the year, giving the house its name. The sun shining through these panels casts a warm glow down to the dome of frescoes directly below—almost like having Christmas lights year round.

Built in 1872 by Colonel Benjamin H. Epperson during Jefferson's heyday, this remarkable mansion is a fine example of architectural transition between Greek Revival and Victorian with a few Italianate characteristics thrown in for good measure. The furnishings, many of which are original to the house, reflect an 1870s Victorian elegance. The current owners, Kirby and Cindy Childress, through creative displays of their own family antiques and heirlooms added to the Epperson furnishings, show their kinship and reverence for this gentle Victorian era.

In addition to the lights and greenery, Kirby and Cindy decorate twenty-eight Christmas trees throughout the different rooms and parlors of the house. Cindy confessed that a few of the trees now remain standing year round because they have run out of storage space! One such tree, completely ornamented with antique family toys, stands upstairs in the children's bedroom. "The Grandmothers' Tree," a tabletop tree in the downstairs Ladies' Parlour, imaginatively displays Cindy's grandmother's teacups and Kirby's grandmother's crocheted decorations hanging amidst a variety of tea bags. Across the hall in the Gentlemen's Parlour, a resplendent 12-foot-tall tree swathed in peach-colored ribbons and ornaments stands beside the magnificently ornate Knabe Concert Grand Piano, which was built for the 1876 Centennial in Philadelphia.

The Seasons Guest House, behind the main house in the reconstructed carriage house, offers bed & breakfast visitors a rare opportunity to enjoy the atmosphere and elegance of gracious Victorian living, complete with a sumptuous breakfast in the splendor of the House of the Seasons main dining room. No matter what the time of year, visitors come away from the House of the Seasons with a warm, nostalgic glow, knowing they have visited a home that is as alive with the past as it is treasured in the present.

The ladies' parlour at House of the Seasons

I have always been a "crafter" and have made different ornaments for the Christmas tree nearly every year since I've been keeping house. As my four children grew up and left to establish their own homes, I presented each of them with a set of the ornaments that I had made while they were children. There was a tiny wreath trimmed with beads and ribbon, hand-crocheted snowflakes, lace angels, candy canes made of twisted ribbon, small lace-trimmed bags of cinnamon potpourri, play-clay gingerbread men, and more. It gave the new young families a head start on their own Christmas decorations and, at the same time, reminded them of their childhood Christmases.

And me? My tree is still adorned with all the ornaments they made for me when they were small. I wouldn't trade the cardboard star covered with glitter (first grade), or the little felt Santa hat (Brownies), or any of the others for all the expensive, fancy decorations in the world.

—PAT SCHUMAN, *Fredericksburg*

Poinsettias
FLORES DE NOCHEBUENA
(FLOWERS OF THE HOLY NIGHT)

For centuries poinsettias have grown wild in Mexico and Central America. Joel Robert Poinsett, the first United States ambassador to Mexico in the early 1800s, became intrigued with the brilliance of this festive, bushlike plant and shipped several to his greenhouse in South Carolina for botanical experimentation when he returned. The plant soon gained popularity there because of its brilliant, seasonal hues, and later became known as a "poinsettia" in his honor.

The Mexican name for the poinsettia, *Flor de Nochebuena* (flower of the Holy Night), derives from an old Mexican legend that tells of a poor child walking to Christmas Eve mass, broken-hearted because she had no gift to take to the baby Jesus. Suddenly an angel of the Lord appeared, saw the child's tears, and instructed her to pick some weeds by the side of the road and take them to the altar. As the story goes, the child offered the tear-soaked weeds to the baby with a simple prayer of love, and miraculously, the weeds burst forth into the brilliant red "blossoms" that have become our joyous holiday symbols.

Glorious poinsettia tree at Lucille Haskell Conservatory in San Antonio

In Texas, searching for the *perfect* poinsettia is becoming almost as popular as finding the perfect Christmas tree. Greenhouses all over the state kick off the holiday season with open houses and festivals that delight both young and old with a glorious array of red, white, pink, and coral poinsettias. On the weekend before Thanksgiving, Ellison's Greenhouse in Brenham holds an **ANNUAL POINSETTIA CELEBRATION** where visitors may revel in the beauty of over 80,000 magnificent plants in 15 varieties. A longtime

Ellison's Greenhouse in Brenham prepares for Christmastime

Ellison's Greenhouse employee says that the most popular varieties are still the reds, but people are starting to enjoy some of the novelty poinsettias like the Sonora Jingle Bell, which has bracts of red and pink and spatters of pink all on the same plant. From the splendor of the towering poinsettia tree, made up of multiple varieties and colors, to the greenhouse tours to Santa Claus, this festive wonderland of activities swirls with color, music, and holiday excitement celebrating these legendary *Flores de Nochebuena.*

Decoration from The Hotel Limpia, Fort Davis

HOMEGROWN CHRISTMAS TREES
by Richard C. Grolla, Houston

Because my wife was allergic to natural evergreen trees, and artificial trees were not available early in our marriage, I began improvising "homegrown" Christmas trees. I remember our first tree was a spur-of-the-moment creation made from stacked hat boxes and green crepe paper. Over the years we tried many things, even once decorating a real yucca plant with lights, balls, and homemade snow. But the yucca spines were killers, and I never tried that again.

For the "growth" of my most successful species, however, I made a frame using a 2 by 2-inch central pole, wooden dowel rods, and cloth strips. Lights were added and papier-mâché foliage applied to the frame. The entire wood and paper tree was then covered with mounded homemade "snow" (made from equal parts of Ivory Flakes and water, whipped with an electric mixer, until it was the consistency of heavy whipped cream). The result, when newly made, was quite beautiful.

These projects were fun, but very time consuming. We now celebrate Christmas with modern, green artificial trees.

I remember Christmas Eve 1948 when we were preparing to have a large family dinner at our house, and our one-year-old daughter pulled over the 9-foot Christmas tree. We sure had a messed-up tree and broken ornaments all over the room that year!

—CLARICE HANSTROM, *Hutto*

Our family's favorite Christmas album is "Muppet Christmas" with John Denver, which we listen to while decorating the tree each year. Our tree has the usual lights, garlands, and tinsel, but what makes it special are the ornaments. The trimming of the tree is a time for telling stories of our past Christmases with each ornament: the "lump" I made in preschool, the ornaments Mom and Dad made the first year they were married, and those my sister and I won or created through the years.

—JENNIFER LATHAM, *Lewisville*

NOEL
V.T. Abercrombie, Houston

Blue spruce, the tree is in the stand,
filling the room with the smell
of Christmas. Smells that track

the past—when tinsel lay crinkled
and heavy on the hand, when bowls
of eggnog shone bright with beads

of sweat, Grandmere directed
decor, quieted arguments that
occasionally broke like ornaments

on the floor, when dolls occupied
spaces under the tree and grownups
smiled secret smiles at me. Tomorrow

we gather, roast turkey scenting the air,
Bloody Marys on silver trays chilling
crystal glasses, stuffed toys,

tricycles bulging under the tree,
chocolate in mugs, loud greetings, hugs,
maybe sharp words, all waiting. And,

waiting, we'll watch the children,
our grandchildren, hold ghosts in
their grasp, begin their long past.

WEST TEXAS TUMBLEWEED CHRISTMAS
by Irma Torres Almager, Midland

As migrants, my family spent holidays in different parts of the state. We traveled around the areas of West Texas following the harvest, so we would usually end up in cotton country for Christmas, always a joyful time for my family.

The connections my father had with the cotton gin owner helped our family of eight take residence in an office building that was too old to use anymore. Somehow, my mother made it a home. It was in this old office building, made out of tin, that we spent one of my most memorable Christmases.

That Christmas I was seven, and my father, as a result of a terrible ginning accident, had been hospitalized for what seemed like an eternity to us kids. With my father in the hospital, we had to be very conservative. Christmas was near and worries of Santa Claus not coming were abundant. Because basic needs always took precedence over holidays, my mother found ways to compensate for what she could not buy. This year was special to me because she chose me to help her locate a Christmas tree.

The empty field across the street from our residence was filled with hundreds of cotton trailers all lined up in rows. We went out and chose the best tumbleweed out of the hundreds that were trapped under the cotton trailers. Mom made choosing one a very special occasion. Once chosen, the tumbleweed was trimmed, cleaned, and taken inside. My mother's fingers bled from the cuts she got while trimming our tree. Then, we watched her decorate it. The next morning our special tumbleweed tree stood on a small table sparkling beautifully. There were no gifts to accompany the tree, but just having it made the day extremely special. Because my dad was ill, it was my mom, my

A rustic Christmas tree creation in Gruene

five brothers and sisters and I against the cruelty that life sometimes brings. In my mind, at age seven, we overcame that cruelty together, as a family.

Reaching for the top in Goliad

I grew up in Cross Plains (about 45 miles from Abilene), and I have many fond memories of cutting down a juniper tree for Christmas each year. I thought the juniper was so full and pretty that I really felt sorry for the rich people who had those scraggly, store-bought trees. We had a few ornaments, but we always strung popcorn and cranberries, too. One year we pulled acorns apart and wrapped the caps in foil—they looked like tiny, silver bells. Our family always put a bird's nest in the branches, too, for good luck. Sometimes we even sprayed the nest gold. But our tree wasn't complete without the icicles. We saved up to buy a new package each year, and then we put it on the tree one strand at a time until the whole tree shimmered.

—DR. MICKEY BUSH, *Sugar Land*

Watson Christmas Tree Farm in Tyler

Christmas Tree Farms

Of all the holiday traditions, the Christmas tree, a custom brought to Texas by early German immigrants, seems to evoke the most nostalgic memories of family fun and togetherness. From selecting a tree, to hanging beloved ornaments, to sitting together in a darkened room enjoying the shimmering array of the decorated tree, the Christmas tree is a family event that embodies the joyousness of the season. Right after Thanksgiving each year, family members gather and begin their quest for this year's "perfect" family tree.

Over fifty Christmas tree farms offer Texas families the old-fashioned adventure and nostalgia of going out together to choose and cut down their own tree for the holidays. What fun it is to be able to circle the trees calling to one another to look at this tree's fullness or another tree's majestic height. Each family member has his or her favorite candidate, which adds to the lively, laughter-filled negotiations. Finally, the family reaches an agreement and the sawing begins, filling the air with that incomparable piney aroma of Christmas.

At most of the Texas farms, however, selecting the tree is just the beginning of the adventure. Watson Christmas Tree Farm in Tyler offers family hay rides, nature walks, and an array of wreaths, herbs, and gifts in addition to tree shaking, flocking, and wrapping. At other farms around the state, children may delight in visiting with Santa Claus, riding a pony, or perhaps petting a variety of animals (even a reindeer or two!). But whatever the activity, the emphasis is on family fun—filling the wellspring of memories for the future.

Our family's favorite tradition is the trip to Piney Woods (East Texas) Christmas Tree Farm on the Friday after Thanksgiving. We pick out the best-shaped, biggest-around spruce we can find in the 15- to 18-foot-tall range. (Yes, really that big!) We then take it to our family's log home and spend two days decorating it with over 7,000 mini-lights. It's a magnificent tree.

—**DOUG BEICH**, *Grand Prairie*

THE CHRISTMAS TREE

V. T. Abercrombie, Houston

Romans exchanged green branches for luck.
Scandinavians worshipped trees.
Germans decorated theirs with cookies, angels, candlelight.
It's remarkable, you can buy light in any grocery
store, pick up Christmas packaged four
to a box, red, green, gold, blue. If a bulb goes
out, you simply replace it. In the olden days, if one

died you screwed them all in and out, over and over,
until you found the burned-out bulb, and then they
glowed, those trees, Douglas firs, Scotch pines, blue
spruce, years of them, at grandmother's, at the house

on Vassar, Locke Lane, Infield, Colquit, Roaring Brook,
Smithdale. Consider that peculiar light that comes
from the tree, a mixture of colors, soft, not a glow,
shadowed with childhoods, tricycles, dolls, skate boards,

eggnog, family quarrels, waiting, late night constructions.
Imagine the sight, imagine the feel, ancestors and friends,
Christmases remembered, passing on the light in the aisle
at the grocery store, with the purchase today, this moment,
of a carton of Christmas tree lights, red, green, gold, blue.

(Published Spring 1998 in *Ilya's Honey*)

One year we were so broke
we made a tree out of chicken
wire and pulled yellow paper
napkins through the wire
leaving a ruffled outside, like
a parade float. Then we hung
lights down the middle of the
inside, put a square of green
satin on the floor and hung
our "tree" from the ceiling!

—JANE CLANCY
DEBENPORT, *Temple*

"THE PERFECT TREE"

by Anice Thompson Vance, Temple

I am a country girl, born and reared in a rural
community. At Christmastime, Daddy would get
his big ax in hand, put us three children in the wagon harnessed to Beck and Kate, our
best mules, and we merrily rocked and bumped to the neighbor's cedar-covered pasture,
since Daddy would not allow cedar to grow on our land. The three of us would run from
one tree to another to make sure we chose the PERFECT one. I can't imagine how many
times we would yell, "Daddy, here it is. Wait, I found a better one!" Now I feel sure that
Daddy had his eye on the perfect one from the start of our search. When a tree was decided
on, we all gathered around it while Daddy chopped and chopped until it fell. Each of us
would take a limb in hand and, with team effort, haul it to the wagon. We were so excited
to call out to Mother as we pulled up to the house, "Mother, come see the perfect Christmas
tree we brought home." Daddy would find pieces of lumber, make a stand, and place the
tree in the living room. We strung popcorn to wrap around the tree, along with paper loops,
which we stuck together with homemade paste Mother had made. My older sister would
melt the wax from the bottom of 4-inch candles to secure them to the strongest tips of the
tree limbs. We were not allowed to burn the candles until Christmas morning, under the
watchful eye of Mother and Daddy. Our most treasured gift Christmas morning was fresh
oranges and apples. My memories of family love, consideration, and togetherness warm
my heart today, seventy-six years later.

Thistle Hill
FORT WORTH

Decked in lavish Victorian and Edwardian holiday elegance, Thistle Hill charms visitors with a delightful glimpse into Texas's turn-of-the-century, cattle baron era. Built in 1903 by Albert Buckman Wharton and his bride, Electra Waggoner (daughter of wealthy rancher W. T. Waggoner), this luxurious Colonial Revival mansion stood in what was known as "Quality Hill," once the most fashionable residential neighborhood in Fort Worth. Electra, reported as one of "Texas's greatest heiresses," became legendary for her flamboyant spending and entertaining, and Thistle Hill (or "Rubusmont," as it was originally named) quickly became the center for lively parties and gatherings.

At Christmas, 1909, Electra's father created his own legend by giving each of his three children and his son-in-law portions of the 595,000-acre family ranch in northwest Texas. For the Whartons' new property, called Sacaweista, W. T. Waggoner also provided cattle and horses, making this amazing Christmas gift worth over two million dollars!

Winfield and Elizabeth Scott were two of the frequent guests at the Thistle Hill parties, and in 1911, when the Whartons decided to sell the mansion and move to their ranch near Vernon, Texas, the Scotts purchased Thistle Hill. They immediately began extensive remodeling to the interior and exterior of the house, which resulted in the elegant Georgian Revival mansion of today. Unfortunately Mr. Scott died in 1911, before the remodeling

Irresistible charm

was completed, but Elizabeth, his widow, and ten-year-old son were able to move into the house the next year.

After Mrs. Scott's death in 1938, the Girl's Service League purchased the mansion, which then served as a supervised residence for young ladies until 1968. For the next seven years Thistle Hill sat vacant, almost swallowed by commercial development in the surrounding area. In 1976, a group of people concerned about historic preservation in the area bought the property from the Girl's Service League and began the restoration efforts.

Today Thistle Hill, uniquely restored so that half the house reflects the Wharton era and half the Scott era, is a self-sustaining house museum and has been featured on the A & E series "America's Castles." At Christmas, the decorations throughout the mansion exemplify the two distinct personalities and styles of Electra Wharton and Elizabeth Scott. From Electra's more flamboyant, rich, dark Victorian ornamentation to Elizabeth's soft pastels and elegant Edwardian touches, Thistle Hill's rooms glow with memories of Fort Worth's Christmas Past.

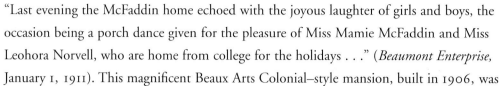

The McFaddin-Ward House

BEAUMONT

"Last evening the McFaddin home echoed with the joyous laughter of girls and boys, the occasion being a porch dance given for the pleasure of Miss Mamie McFaddin and Miss Leohora Norvell, who are home from college for the holidays . . ." (*Beaumont Enterprise,* January 1, 1911). This magnificent Beaux Arts Colonial–style mansion, built in 1906, was

McFaddin-Ward entry hall decked out nicely for the Christmas season

home to the wealthy Beaumont business leader W. P. H. McFaddin and his wife, Ida Caldwell McFaddin, who hosted many such gala occasions during the first half of the twentieth century. Today, holiday decorations closely resemble the Christmas "dress" of that bygone era of splendor, thanks to the many detailed newspaper reports and diary entries of Mrs. McFaddin and her daughter, Mamie McFaddin-Ward.

Poinsettias (six dozen, according to Mrs. Ward's 1940 diary), mistletoe, moss, evergreen garlands, and huge quantities of fresh cut flowers adorned the entry hall and every room of the house—the perfect setting for the eggnog parties, open houses, and other gala occasions that the McFaddins and Wards traditionally held between Christmas and New Year's. Now, holiday visitors can step back in time and enjoy delightful glimpses of that elegant past, especially evident in the dining room which is set for a holiday reception as reported in the January 2, 1916, *Beaumont Daily Journal:* "The dining room was treated with warm red tints, the table being topped with big bows of wide satin ribbon and red carnations in crystal vases. Streamers and bows of red maline and candles of the same bright color completed the effect of gaiety and festivity."

Banks of poinsettias also add a special holiday glow to the warmth and intimacy of the nearby breakfast room/conservatory—one of the most unique rooms in the house, featuring fabulous art glass windows. Every room features so many nostalgic reminders of the McFaddin and Ward families and the gracious hospitality extended to their guests that it almost seems possible to hear the distant clink of glasses or a low rumble of laughter echoing from those long-ago parties!

Breakfast room and Conservatory ready for the holiday visitors

Mamie McFaddin-Ward treasured her home and took great care to preserve her family's unique collection of furnishings. Before she died in 1982, she created the Mamie McFaddin-Ward Foundation to maintain the house as a museum—not as a family "shrine," but as an example of the life and culture of an early twentieth-century southeast Texas family. Today, the McFaddin-Ward Foundation preserves and maintains the museum as a rich resource center, fulfilling Mamie's dreams of her home continuing to serve the community.

McFADDIN-WARD HOUSE EGGNOG

12 egg whites

3 quarts milk

½ cup cream

4 cups sugar

¼ tsp. salt

2 Tbsp. vanilla

⅓ cup rum (optional)

Beat egg whites for 3 minutes. Gradually pour in the milk and cream. Add sugar, salt, and vanilla. Let stand 10 minutes to thoroughly dissolve the sugar. Stir several times. Add rum. Chill.

Yield: 18 portions

—*from* **PERFECTLY SPLENDID** *The McFaddin-Ward House Cookbook*
used by permission of McFaddin-Ward Foundation

Texas-sized cowboy boots at North Star Mall in San Antonio

This has been a favorite family appetizer for years!

—JOY GRAHAM

Rosevine Inn, Tyler's first bed & breakfast, is built on the foundation where a large English Tudor mansion once stood. It is located in the historic Brick Street District of Tyler. Delicious formal breakfasts, including orange muffins, in the main dining room delight visitors year round.

—REBECCA POWELL

FETA CHEESE DIP OR SPREAD

4 oz. feta cheese, softened
¼ of 8 oz. pkg. cream cheese
   (regular or fat-free), softened
1 clove garlic, minced
⅓ cup mayonnaise

⅛ tsp. thyme, crushed
¼ tsp. dried basil
¼ tsp. dried oregano
⅛ tsp. dill weed

Combine feta cheese, cream cheese, mayonnaise, and garlic. Mix well. Add herbs and mix well. Chill. Serve with crackers as spread or with chips.

—LOLA BURGESS, *Silsbee*

SPICY CHEESE DIP

2 lb. Velveeta cheese
1 can hot Rotel tomatoes/chilies

1 lb. spicy pork sausage
1 sm. can hot chilies

Melt Velveeta, using just enough milk to reach your desired consistency. Fry sausage until crumbled and done; drain well. Add sausage to Velveeta; add drained Rotel and drained chilies. Stir to mix, then serve with your favorite chips or vegetable pieces.

Variations: Can also be made with hot Italian sausage.

—SALLY SOBEY, *San Antonio*

BUFFALO WINGS

18 to 20 chicken wings,
   cut into separate pieces
½ cup sugar

½ cup water
⅓ cup soy sauce

Mix sugar, water, and soy sauce until dissolved. Lay wing portions into liquid mixture in a covered frying pan or an electric skillet. Cook over medium to low heat for 40 minutes to 1 hour. Liquid becomes sticky and cooks away. Turn or stir frequently.

—JOY GRAHAM, *Thorndale*

ORANGE MUFFINS

¾ cup cooking oil
1 cup sugar
2 eggs
1½ cups flour
1 tsp. salt

1 tsp. baking soda
1 tsp. vanilla
¼ cup fresh orange juice
2 Tbsp. grated orange rind

Combine oil, sugar, and eggs. Mix well. Add remaining ingredients. Blend. Pour into muffin pan sprayed with Pam. Bake at 350° F for 10–15 minutes.

I glaze my muffins with ½ cup powdered sugar mixed with about 1 Tbsp. orange juice.

—REBECCA POWELL, *Tyler, Rosevine Inn Bed and Breakfast*

ARMADILLO EGGS

30 jalepenos
2–3 cups Bisquick
1 lb. sausage

1 lb. Monterey Jack cheese
1 small can chopped green chilies
1 envelope Shake 'n Bake for pork

Cut jalepenos in half and de-seed them. Set aside. Mix remaining ingredients. Form small patties using sausage mixture, and fold a patty around each jalepeno half. Roll in Shake 'n Bake. Bake at 400° F about 25 minutes or until lightly brown.

—LEESA EKLUND, *Sealy*

Plum Pudding Party

As our three daughters began to grow up, Christmas Day, after opening presents, needed some pepping up, so we began the tradition of inviting friends over for our Plum Pudding Party on Christmas night. Decorating the table, arranging the food, and serving our guests extended the joy of Christmas for us all. None of our guests want to miss the lighting of the brandy to pour over the first pudding (and each successive pudding!).

PLUM PUDDING

3 cups bread crumbs

1 cup each—black raisins, yellow raisins, currants, and citron

1⅓ cups sugar

1 tsp. each—cinnamon, mace, and nutmeg

2 sticks butter, melted

4 large eggs, lightly beaten

a few drops of almond extract

½ cup orange marmalade

¼ cup cognac

Toss raisins, spices, and bread crumbs. Add melted butter and toss again. Add remaining ingredients and toss again. Grease a pudding pan and sprinkle with sugar. Pack pudding mixture into pan, filling about ⅔ full. Cover with a round of wax paper and lid. One recipe fills a large pudding pan or two smaller ones.

Place the pudding on a trivet in a kettle and add enough water to reach about a third of the way up the pan. Heat to simmer and let steam about 6 hours. Pudding is done when it is a dark brown color and firm to the touch.

Let the pudding cool in its container. Store in the refrigerator; pudding will keep several months.

To serve: Reheat pudding in steamer until quite warm. Unmold onto a hot serving plate. Pour hot rum or brandy around the pudding and ignite. Serve with hard sauce.

HARD SAUCE

⅓ cup butter

1 cup powdered sugar

1 Tbsp. cognac (amount of cognac varies with individual taste)

Mix butter and powdered sugar until it reaches the consistency of paste; stir in cognac.

—MARY JANE REEVES, *Canyon*

EERDBEERN BOWLE

1 pint good cognac

3 fifths dry white wine
 (use champagne for a wedding party)

1½ to 3 lb. strawberries with drawn juice

a generous lb. of sugar

1 cup sparkling water

Soak berries, sugar, and cognac together for 4–6 hours. Just before serving, add wine, all at once, plus 1 cup sparkling water. Serve at room temperature or chilled.

—MARY JANE REEVES, *Canyon*

One of my favorite holiday traditions is to invite friends to a custard party. I serve the custard in the fanciest cups in the china cabinet. Guests may add a dollop of whipped cream and sprinkle nutmeg over the top (and maybe even a little sherry). Men usually want a large cup to add bourbon! Trays of fruitcake, fancy cookies, and toasted nuts round out the menu for a delightful time with friends.

—MARGUERITE STARR CRAIN, *Midland*

My husband and I have certainly enjoyed the Reeves' annual Plum Pudding Party. They send out invitations in lieu of Christmas cards to local people—"from seven o'clock 'til the pudding's gone." The pudding is ignited, and I am sure the punch could ignite, too!

—NELL FINDLEY, *Canyon*

A recipe given to us thirty-five years ago by Dr. and Mrs. Cykler, originally for the weddings of our daughters.

—MARY JANE REEVES

The spirit of the season at Salado Square

PACHANGA CORN SALSA

2 ears of cooked shucked corn
1 diced red onion
1 diced green pepper
1 cup green tomatoes or tomatillos
1 small peeled and diced ripe avocado
1 tsp. minced garlic
1 tsp. or more diced jalapeno pepper

1 Tbsp. red wine vinegar
1 Tbsp. vegetable oil
1 tsp. ground cumin
1 tsp. chili powder
juice of 2 limes
salt, pepper, Cholula or Tabasco to taste

All diced ingredients should be cut to ⅜" size.

Boil corn for 10 minutes. Remove from heat and let cool for 5 minutes. (Alternate method of cooking corn: Microwave for 6 minutes in the shucks. This is the best way to cook corn on the cob anyway!) Cut corn from cob and combine with the other ingredients. Cover and refrigerate for 3–4 hours. Makes 2 cups. Delicious!!

—RAOUL NACHI, *San Antonio*

CRAB DIP

1 can cream of mushroom soup
1 package (8 oz.) cream cheese
1 package gelatin
¼ cup cool water
½ cup chopped green onion

½ cup chopped celery
1 cup mayonnaise
¼ tsp. curry
1 package lump crabmeat (or imitation)

Heat soup and stir in cheese until completely blended. Add gelatin and stir. Stir in remaining ingredients—blend thoroughly. Pour into lightly greased mold and refrigerate for 4 hours. To serve: Unmold and serve with crackers.

—CHRIS SCHAVRDA, *Sealy*

SOUTH TEXAS CHILI CON QUESO

1 medium yellow onion
6 Tbsp. butter or vegetable oil
½ cup whole milk or cream
1 lb. Velveeta cheese, cut into 1-inch cubes

1 lb. Monterey Jack cheese, cut into one-inch cubes
1 can Rotel tomatoes or 1 cup pico de gallo

Dice onion and sauté in butter until translucent. Add milk and both cheeses and stir constantly over medium heat until cheese melts. Stir in Rotel tomatoes until blended. Keep hot in double boiler or transfer to a crock pot on low heat setting.

—RICHARD REYNOLDS, *Austin*

GUACAMOLE

6 avocados
1 tsp. prepared habanero or Tabasco sauce
½ cup diced tomato
8 scallions, chopped

¼ cup chopped cilantro
juice of one lime or lemon
salt to taste

Halve each avocado, remove pits and scoop into a large bowl. Mash with a fork, leaving slightly chunky. Add remaining ingredients and stir until well mixed. Season to taste with salt. Serve immediately as a dip or garnish.

—RICHARD REYNOLDS, *Austin*

Parlor with exotic Oriental touches

Mr. De's library

The DeGolyer House

DALLAS

On the shores of White Rock Lake, surrounded by the Dallas Arboretum and Botanical Gardens, the distinctive DeGolyer House brightens the Metroplex holiday scene as Dallas' foremost interior designers work their holiday magic throughout the 21,000 square-foot mansion. With a different theme each year, the designers creatively transform this Spanish Colonial Revival-style mansion with festive holiday splendor, much to the delight of all those who tour during "Holiday at the Arboretum." For 1998's theme, "Mystical & Magical Colors of the Orient," parasols, dragons, and numerous Oriental artifacts and accessories decorated mantels, trees and fireplaces, giving the DeGolyer House an exotic holiday touch.

Everette DeGolyer (Mr. De), often called the father of geophysical exploration, and his wife, Nell, built the mansion in 1939-40, choosing a design that reflected their penchant for entertaining as well as awareness of their location. The irregular plan takes full advantage of the lake view and was also laid out to accommodate existing trees and plants, which subsequently became part of the gardens. House contractor, Al Holmberg, reportedly had to reposition the house four times to save trees and plants.

The DeGolyers wanted the mansion to look 100 years old upon completion as illustrated by the coffered ceiling in the parlor and the heavy oak sixteenth-century antiques throughout the house. Of the mansion's 13 rooms, the magnificent library with its floor-to-ceiling shelves of books best reflects Mr. De's personality and love of books and was probably considered the heart of the house during the 1940s and 1950s to the DeGolyers' steady stream of influential visitors.

Christmas at the DeGolyer House continues to grow and evolve, making the Dallas Arboretum and Botanical Gardens a delightful holiday retreat away from the harried pace of the city.

*Overleaf:
The arms of
a mesquite
tree bend over
prickly pear
in Enchanted
Rock State
Natural Area,
Gillespie*

Dickens on the Strand carolers

Galveston's Dickens on the Strand

For over twenty-five years, visiting Galveston's Strand National Historic Landmark District on the first weekend in December is like stepping into a bustling, nineteenth-century London scene straight from a Dickens novel. Hoop-skirted ladies stroll the garland-draped streets beside their frock-coated escorts. Street urchins sneak food from unsuspecting street vendors. English bobbies direct passersby to "Piccadilly Circus" and "Trafalgar Square" while many a Scrooge and Tiny Tim wander through the crowd enjoying the continuous entertainment on street corners and various stages scattered throughout the nine-block area. Anyone who comes dressed in Victorian costume gets free admission and literally becomes part of the show for the largest annual holiday festival in Texas. Both Saturday's and Sunday's schedules feature costume contests that further encourage participants to create the perfect Victorian or Dickens-era costumes.

The Strand, once a thriving financial district known as the Wall Street of the Southwest, is one of the finest examples of Victorian architecture in this country. The ornate, iron-front buildings, reminiscent of London's Strand, set the scene perfectly for this Victorian-style Christmas festival. Not even the original Ebeneezer Scrooge himself could muster a "Bah, Humbug" on this weekend filled with parades, street performers, jugglers, magicians, handbell ringers, carolers, and bagpipers. The youngest "chimney sweep" to the most majestic Queen Victoria, after starting the holiday season at Dickens on the Strand, can exclaim with Tiny Tim, "God bless us every one!"

Ashton Villa
GALVESTON

Holiday garlands and wreaths grace the stately, Italianate facade of Ashton Villa, built in 1859 by wealthy hardware merchant James Moreau Brown. Ashton Villa enjoys the distinction of being the *first* of Galveston's brick mansions and the *first* Italianate-design house in Texas, as well as one of the most expensive houses of its day, surpassing even the Governor's Mansion in Austin. By the 1870s and 1880s, the Browns also held *firsts* in lavish entertainment, especially on New Year's Day, which was considered the most festive day of the year in Galveston.

Miss Bettie, the Browns' oldest daughter, caused many a stir in Galveston society by flaunting all the usual rules for a nineteenth-century woman. She turned down every proposal of marriage; she smoked cigarettes and occasionally a pipe; she traveled unchaperoned on many ocean cruises; and she went to Europe to study art! Despite her reputation, Miss Bettie's invitations were highly sought after; no one ever turned down an opportunity to see the latest fashions and outrageous ideas she brought back from her many travels.

Having withstood the ravages of time, weather, and man-made changes, Ashton Villa is now the oldest remaining antebellum mansion on Broadway and is listed on the National Register of Historic Places. The Galveston Historical Foundation has undertaken meticulous restoration that allows today's visitors the opportunity to step into the gilded Victorian era.

Now during the Christmas season, evergreen garlands and bright bows adorn banisters and mantels throughout the villa, and an elegant, 12-foot Christmas tree fills the parlor with Victorian splendor. Upstairs, smaller trees adorn the family quarters, and historic toys displayed in the children's bedroom conjure up visions of childhood for visitors of all ages. A grand Dickens Feast held in the villa's ballroom during Dickens on the Strand often features Mark Charles Dickens, the great, great grandson of Charles Dickens, who gives spirited readings from A Christmas Carol between courses of the sumptuous meal. Ashton Villa also welcomes Saturday morning Dickens visitors to a splendid morning tea in the best English tradition, complete with seasonal music and a tour of the lavishly decorated mansion . . . hopefully up to Miss Bettie's standards!

Elegant dining at Ashton Villa

My most memorable Christmas in Texas is the one when I came back to Texas to live. I was born in Victoria, Texas, but my father was in the Air Force, so we traveled a lot. Then I married a wonderful guy in the Navy, and again we traveled a lot. When my husband retired in 1997, we came back to Texas to live. It was so nice to be with all of my family again and also to be in Texas and NOT where the snow was up to our knees!

— **KATHY LEE**, *Brookshire*

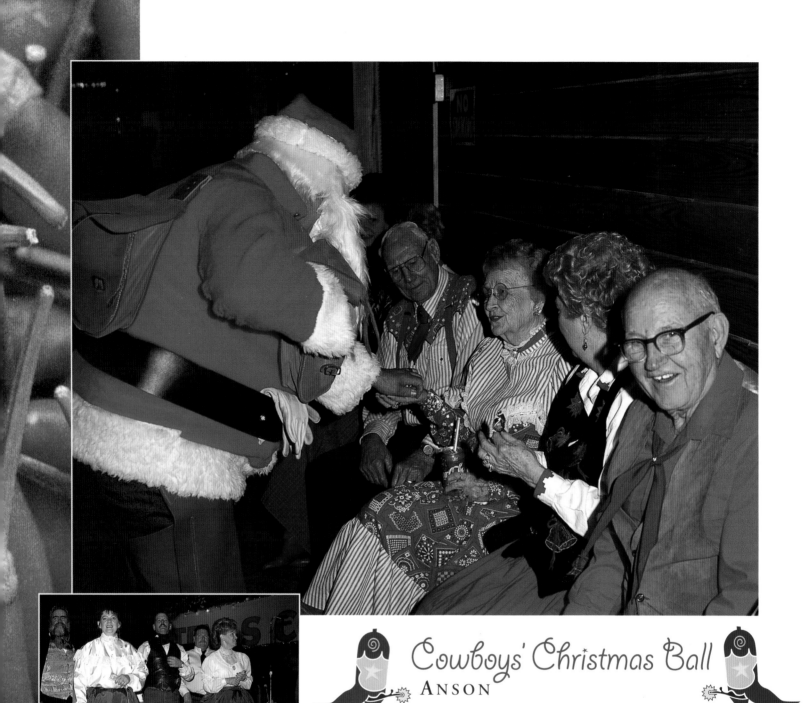

Cowboys' Christmas Ball
ANSON

Every year on the weekend before Christmas, the little West Texas town of Anson opens the doors of Pioneer Hall (built specially for the occasion) and throws a real boot-stompin', fiddle-scrapin', *"lively gaited sworray"* known as the *Cowboys' Christmas Ball*. This ball had its beginnings in 1885 when Morning Star Hotel proprietor M. C. Rhoads sent word to all the cowhands in the area that there would be "great doings" at the hotel in Anson the Saturday night before Christmas. And come to Anson they did. In fact, the ball was such a hit with all the cowhands and the ladies in the territory that it became a yearly event.

Along about 1890, as the story goes, a young easterner named Larry Chittenden wandered into town to check on his uncle's ranch land and was asked to attend the ball. He was so impressed with the festivities that he later penned the words to the poem "The Cowboys' Christmas Ball," immortalizing the event as well as his own place in Texas folklore history. His colorful language and descriptions, just as true today as in the 1890s, show the real flavor of this ball:

The dust riz fast an' furious, we all just
galloped 'round,
Till the scenery got so giddy, that Z Bar
Dick was downed.
We buckled on our partners, an' tole 'em
to hold on,
Then shook our hoofs like lightning,
until the early dawn.

No wonder the *"boys had left their ranches and come to town in piles,"* and *"The Ladies kinda scatterin', had gathered in for miles."* Who could resist a chance to do the Virginia reel or the Cotton-eyed Joe with *"the music sighin', an' a-wailin' through the hall."*

Chittenden's poem sparked a movement to revive the annual ball at Anson. Now local residents declare, "It just wouldn't be Christmas without the Cowboys' Christmas Ball!" Each year the Pioneer Hall is decked out with mountain cedar, antlers, and cattle horn relics, interlaced with festoons of holiday decorations. Promptly at eight o'clock, frontier-garbed hosts and hostesses welcome guests from all directions—some even as far away as California! "It's really like a big reunion," says one veteran dancer. But amidst all the dancing and visiting, everyone keeps an ear cocked to catch the orchestra's first strains of

"The Eyes of Texas." With this song, the spirited Grand March, led by couples who have married since the last ball, swings into action, and *The Cowboys' Christmas Ball* is officially "on."

Santa pays a visit to the Ball in Anson

The Cowboys' Christmas Ball

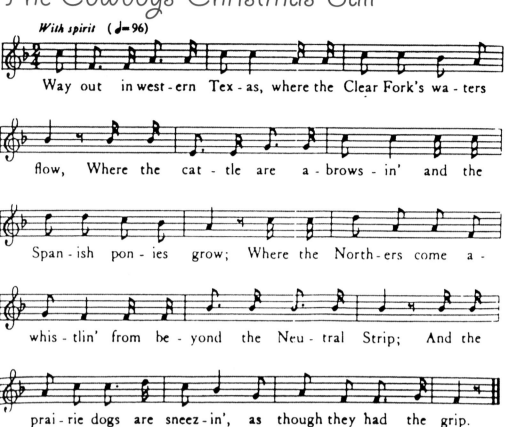

With spirit (♩=96)

Way out in west-ern Tex-as, where the Clear Fork's wa-ters

flow, Where the cat-tle are a-brows-in' and the

Span-ish pon-ies grow; Where the North-ers come a-

whis-tlin' from be-yond the Neu-tral Strip; And the

prai-rie dogs are sneez-in', as though they had the grip.

Where the coyotes come a-howlin' round the ranches after dark,
And the mockin' birds are singin' to the lovely medder lark;
Where the 'possum and the badger and the rattlesnakes abound,
And the monstrous stars are winkin' o'er a wilderness profound;

Where lonesome, tawny prairies melt into airy streams,
While the Double Mountains slumber in heavenly kinds of dreams;
Where the antelope is grazin' and the lonely plovers call—
It was there I attended the Cowboys' Christmas Ball.

The town was Anson City, old Jones's county seat,
Where they raised Polled Angus cattle and waving whiskered wheat;
Where the air is soft and bammy and dry and full of health,
Where the prairies is explodin' with agricultural wealth;

Where they print the *Texas Western,* that Hec McCann supplies,
With news and yarns and stories, of most amazing size;
Where Frank Smith "pulls the badger" on knowing tenderfeet,
And Democracy's triumphant and mighty hard to beat;

Where lives that good old hunter, John Milsay from Lamar,
Who used to be the sheriff "back east in Paris, sah"!
'Twas there, I say, at Anson with the lovely Widder Wall,
That I went to that reception, the Cowboys' Christmas Ball.

The boys had left their ranches and come to town in piles;
The ladies, kinda scatterin', had gathered in for miles.
And yet the place was crowded, as I remember well,
'Twas gave on this occasion at the Morning Star Hotel.

The music was a fiddle and a lively tambourine,
And a viol came imported, by the stage from Abilene.
The room was togged out gorgeous—with mistletoe
  and shawls,
And the candles flickered festious, around the airy walls.

The wimmen folks looked lovely—the boys looked
  kinder treed,
Till the leader commenced yelling, "Whoa, fellers,
  let's stampede,"
And the music sighin', an' a-wailin' through the hall
As a kind of introduction to the Cowboys' Christmas Ball.

The leader was a feller that came from Swenson's ranch—
They called him Windy Billy from Little Deadman's Branch.
His rig was kinder keerless—big spurs and high-heeled boots;
He had the reputation that comes when a feller shoots.

His voice was like the bugle upon the mountain height;
His feet were animated, and a mighty movin' sight,
When he commenced to holler, "Now, fellers, shake your pen!
Lock horns ter all them heifers and rustle them like men;

"Saloot yer lovely critters; neow swing and let 'em go;
Climb the grapevine round 'em; neow all hands do-ce-do!
You maverick, jine the round-up—jes' skip the waterfall,"
Huh! Hit was getting active, the Cowboys' Christmas Ball.

The boys was tolerable skittish, the ladies powerful neat,
That old bass viol's music just got there with both feet!
That wailin', frisky fiddle, I never shall forget;
And Windy kept a-singin'—I think I hear him yet—

"Oh, X's, chase yer squirrels, and cut 'em to our side;
Spur Treadwell to the center, with Cross P Charley's bride,
Doc Hollis down the center, and twine the ladies' chain,
Van Andrews, pen the fillies in big T Diamond's train."

"All pull your freight together, neow swallow fork and change;
Big Boston, lead the trail herd through little Pitchfork's range.
Purr round yer gentle pussies, neow rope and balance all!"
Huh! Hit were gettin' active—the Cowboys' Christmas Ball.

The dust riz fast and furious; we all jes' galloped round,
Till the scenery got so giddy that T Bar Dick was downed.
We buckled to our partners and told 'em to hold on,
Then shook our hoofs like lightning until the early dawn.

Don't tell me 'bout cotillions or Germans. No, sir-ee!
That whirl at Anson City jes' takes the cake with me.
I'm sick of lazy shufflin's, of them I've had my fill,
Give me a frontier breakdown backed up by Windy Bill.

McAllister ain't nowhere, when Windy leads the show;
I've seen 'em both in harness and so I ought ter know.
Oh, Bill, I shan't forget yer, and I oftentimes recall
That lively gaited sworray—the Cowboys' Christmas Ball.

Collected, adapted and arranged by John A. Lomax and Alan Lomax
TRO - © 1938 (Renewed) Ludlow Music, Inc., New York, NY. Used by permission.

The Governor's Mansion
AUSTIN

During the first week in December, the air crackles with holiday excitement as a white, horse-drawn carriage, laden with Christmas trees for Texas's First Family, pulls up to the stately, Greek Revival–style Governor's Mansion. Governor George W. Bush is on hand to give his nod of approval as the trees, selected by the Texas Christmas Tree Growers Association, are brought in and readied for his family to decorate.

*Parlor mirror reflects the elegance
of the Governor's Mansion tree*

Outside, the mansion also takes on a holiday glow with festive swags of lighted holiday greenery draped gracefully from the elegant double galleries, poinsettias adorning the front steps, and Texas-sized, gaily wrapped presents overflowing from the bright red sleigh parked on the lawn. Just down the hill from the Governor's Mansion, at the intersection of 11th and Congress in front of the Capitol building, the last decorations are hung on

the 27-foot Texas cedar in preparation for Governor Bush's official lighting ceremony the first weekend in December.

The Governor's Mansion, the fourth oldest in the United States, has been home to Texas's first families since 1856 when Austin master builder Abner Cook completed this elegant mansion (funded by $17,000 of state appropriated funds) for Governor Elisha Pease and his family. Since then, each Texas governor has filled the mansion with his or her unique contributions to its preservation as well as personal family traditions and history.

Texas's First Lady, Laura Bush, continues this tradition by sharing some of her family's holiday memories:

Governor's Mansion decoration

TEXAS CHRISTMAS
by Laura Bush

One thing about Texans: we are a generous lot, especially during the holiday season. Whether it's looking after a neighbor in need, telling a tall tale about the Christmas tree that got away, or passing along the recipe for our favorite feast, there isn't much we wouldn't love to share with our friends. With that in mind, I offer you a favorite holiday story and recipe.

For my family, Christmas always evokes warm memories of sipping steaming cups of hot chocolate with our twin daughters, Barbara and Jenna. I'll never forget one holiday season, after decorating our tree, I told the girls—who were little children at the time—to sit under the Christmas tree, and I would bring them some hot chocolate. When I returned from the kitchen, I found them struggling to obey my instructions. They were sitting Indian-style, doubled over and nearly buried under the limbs at the base of the tree. Alas! At age three they took our words literally; at seventeen, they take our words with a grain of salt.

OLD-FASHIONED HOT CHOCOLATE

1 quart of milk
3 Tbsp. granulated sugar
3 Tbsp. cocoa powder

2 tsp. vanilla extract
¼ tsp. cinnamon
a pinch of salt

In a mixing bowl, blend cocoa, sugar, cinnamon, and salt. Set aside. Heat milk in a heavy saucepan; remove from heat before it simmers. Add 1 cup of the warm milk and vanilla to the dry mixture; whisk until smooth and pour mixture into the pan of warm milk. Continue to heat and whisk until frothy, being careful not to scorch. Pour into mugs and, as an option, top with miniature marshmallows and stir with a candy cane.

There's something about Christmastime that makes George and me marvel at how our girls have grown. Perhaps it is because we remember them as little children, when they delighted in filling the first few feet of tree limbs (as high as they could stretch!) with hand-made ornaments. Year by year, branch by branch, the ornaments have moved up the tree, and our children have grown into fine young women. Now, much to George's dismay, they can reach the upper limbs as easily as their father!

One thing we know for certain: the more things change with each passing Christmas, the more we appreciate our family traditions. This year, after we finish trimming our tree in the Governor's Mansion, you will find us all toasting our success with a cup of Old-Fashioned Hot Chocolate.

Christmas Strolls

Picture trees glittering with thousands of lights. Imagine bejeweled historic courthouses and town squares. Add strolling carolers, buggy rides, live nativity scenes, holiday foods, dancers, and Santa Claus, of course. Then invite family, friends, and all of Texas to enjoy this good old-fashioned community "wing-ding," and you have all the ingredients for a Texas-style Christmas Stroll set in Salado, Brenham, Georgetown, Seguin, or any one of a dozen other towns across the state.

The Brenham Stroll starts off my Christmas season with a wonderful sense of community as friends and neighbors greet each other and take the time to visit and enjoy the lights, decorations, carols, and joys of the season together.

—LADONNA VEST, *Independence*

Glowing luminarias line the main streets of Salado, ushering thousands of visitors into a fairyland of white, twinkling lights during the two weekends of the annual SALADO CHRISTMAS STROLL. This community-wide event combines people and talent from all over Central Texas in a spectacular holiday extravaganza. On Main Street, local actors from Salado's own Table Rock Theater stage vignettes from their annual production of Dickens's *A Christmas Carol* while carolers stroll through the village entertaining visitors with the delightful strains of traditional Christmas carols. Potpourri-scented specialty and antique shops, which make Salado a shopper's paradise any time of year, teem with holiday cheer and magical gift ideas. Sleigh bells jingle in time to the horse's clip-clopping as a buggy full of revelers tours the holiday-studded streets. Crowds gather at the First Baptist Church to witness a live nativity each evening of the first weekend. For 1998's stroll theme, "The Twelve Days of Christmas," local artists created twelve large murals (one for each day), which dotted the half mile of Salado's main street like giant Christmas cards and will likely become standard "greetings" for future Salado Christmas Strolls.

Christmas-wrapped children add to the joy of the Georgetown Stroll

Dozens of 6-foot-tall, sparkling angels add celestial glow to the annual BRENHAM CHRISTMAS STROLL festivities around the historic Washington County Courthouse Square outlined in thousands of holiday lights. Merchants around the square stay open late and deck their shops in holiday splendor, offering the perfect gifts for any Santa's list. Brenham residents say they "look forward to this event because it brings people together in the downtown area to relax, do a little shopping, enjoy the entertainment, and visit with friends while nibbling on an array of holiday goodies."

Magical gift ideas abound at Sir Wigglesworth during the Salado Stroll

Enjoying the Salado Stroll

A festive parade followed by a candle lighting ceremony highlights the GEORGETOWN CHRISTMAS STROLL, which draws family and friends to historic, downtown Williamson County Courthouse Square. Good food, good friends, a parade, and a multitude of activities for kids of all ages add to the splendor of the Christmas decorations and music, providing the necessary ingredients for this annual romp down holiday lane. One longtime resident says the *Christmas Stroll* always reminds him of the '30s when he and his friends would "come in to town on Saturday night and 'cadillac' around the square to impress the girls." Now the stroll is really one of the few opportunities for people to gather around the square and fellowship with one another.

Gayle Leonard and Santa at The Dusty Rose in Salado

My first Christmas in Texas was in 1993. We moved to Mansfield and for the first time in ten years all five of my children and their spouses were together for a very rowdy Christmas. We all love Mansfield's Christmas in the Park—it's a great way to get in the "Christmas Mood."

—LINDA WILSON, *Mansfield*

A pleasant respite in Salado

SEGUIN adds a creative twist to their *"Holiday Stroll in Central Park"* with *Living Windows*—live tableaus with costumed participants acting out various turn-of-the-century family Christmas scenes in eight lighted windows of the downtown business storefronts. In one window, the Seguin Garden Club portrays a country Christmas theme featuring people knitting, crocheting, and stringing popcorn. They report that the most difficult part is NOT looking back at the people outside the window! These poignant glimpses of Christmas past add to the holiday parade and arrival of Santa Claus, downtown lighting, and Victorian refreshments, filling Seguin's cup of Christmas cheer to overflowing.

Whatever the theme, location, or entertainment, the Christmas Stroll brings each community together at the beginning of December to celebrate the old-fashioned joys of the Christmas season as well as honoring their rich historical heritage.

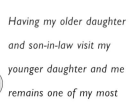

Having my older daughter and son-in-law visit my younger daughter and me remains one of my most memorable Christmases. We went to see a local production of "Scrooge" and visited the Whitehead Memorial Museum to see the Codera Nativity Exhibit—an entire building depicting the Christmas Story with a collection of figurines and tiny trees and buildings. Then we went to the midnight church service together.

—SUSAN COTTLE LEONARD, *Del Rio*

Our town of Brownfield has a Christmas Home Tour every year. There are usually four homes on the tour and a business where refreshments are served. The people decorate their own homes and the business provides the food. Proceeds from ticket sales are used for scholarships and community needs.

—LEE WISE, *Brownfield*

Every Christmas season, sporadically placed neighbors up and down our country road get together and have a progressive Christmas party. Four families volunteer to host a segment of our dinner party in their home. On that special evening, we go from house to house enjoying champagne and appetizers, soup and salad, and wine and entree and then finish up with a scrumptious dessert. It's a wonderful way to share the Christmas spirit of love with our neighbors.

—KAREN GOTCHER, *Fredericksburg*

St. John's Church at Sam Houston Park

Candlelight Tour in Sam Houston Park

Houston, second week in December

Nestled in the heart of downtown Houston under the watchful eyes of twentieth-century glass and steel sky-scrapers, Sam Houston Park, home to eight of the city's oldest structures, rings in the holiday season with a delightful tour of Houston's Christmas Past. Each house, decked out for its own era, brims with excitement and activity as costumed members of the Heritage Society portray lively family scenes and re-create parties of yore. Candlelight, cups of steaming wassail, strolling carolers—all this and more as *Candlelight* visitors begin their nostalgic holiday tour.

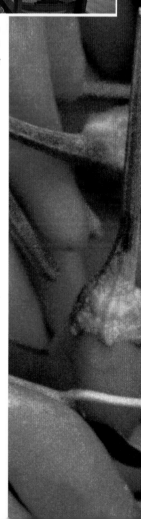

From the simple, one-room **Old Place,** built in 1824, the walkway candles provide a glowing path toward **The Pillot House,** built in 1868 and adorned with lavish, mid-Victorian holiday decorations that reflect the family's French heritage.

In a traditional, late nineteenth-century German household, Christmas meant food and family and Old World decorations, as found in **San Felipe Cottage,** home to Justina and William Ruppersberg in the late 1860s. Visitors delight in seeing the antique turkey feather Christmas tree (made up of feathers wound onto branches—a tradition in Germany begun for forest conservation) with its elaborate nativity scene (putz) underneath.

On the verandah of **Staiti House,** built in 1905, choristers fill the night air with lilting strains of madrigals and carols, ushering visitors into the lavish home of Houston oil pioneer Henry T. Staiti. In a delightful blend of traditional holiday greenery and wedding finery, the downstairs of the seventeen-room house portrays a 1920 family Christmas wedding.

Living room of the Staiti House

The bride poses in the living room for pre-wedding photographs, the dining room table holds a bountiful reception feast, and a Christmas tree twinkles with "modern" electric lights (the only "electrified" tree in the park) on the adjacent sunporch.

Leaving the Staiti House, strollers walk up the path and into the simpler times of **Yates House,** home of Reverend John Henry Yates, who was freed on "Juneteenth" (June 19, 1865) and became known for his help in leading his congregation and community from slavery to civic esteem on the 1870s.

Across the lawn from Yates House, the voices of the Houston Boys Choir fill the tiny, hundred-year-old **St. John's Church** with glorious sounds of Christmas past and present. This German Lutheran Church, originally built in Northwest Harris County, is typical of the churches that dotted the late nineteenth-century rural landscape. Lit with flickering kerosene lamps and decorated with native Texas greenery and a wonderful tree covered with white paper cutouts made by Sunday School children, St. John's radiates the simple joys of the season.

No Candlelight in the Park tour would be complete without visiting the **Nichols-Rice-Cherry House,** once the home of William Marsh Rice (for whom Rice University was named). A party, much like one of the Rices' famous holiday gatherings, is in progress and Candlelight visitors are the special guests.

Carolers on the second-story balcony welcome visitors to nearby **Kellum-Noble House,** which has the distinction of being the only structure in the park on its original location as well as being the oldest residential structure in Houston on its original site. This home, built in the late 1840s, was once part of the Houston Public School system, with Zerviah Noble, second owner of the house, as teacher.

Back at the park's museum, visitors can enjoy steaming mugs of wassail, listen to lively Christmas music, and marvel at the old-time craft demonstrations, such as weaving, lace-making, and woodcarving. As the evening ends and the candles around the walkways are extinguished, Candlelight visitors must return to their teeming, modern-day schedules, but they take with them cherished echoes from over one hundred years of Christmas in Houston.

The church at Dubina (below), the first Czech-Moravian settlement in Texas, has uncovered, during recent restorations, some of the original designs of angels around the tops of pillars. From these and other originals, the parish was able to make stencils and repaint the inside of the church, giving the nearly 200 people attending weekly services a sense of connection with their heritage.

St. Mary's at High Hill (above), with its 175-foot-high steeple, still holds services for its parishioners, many of whom are descendants of the original German and Czech settlers. Some of the original painted wall decorations have been covered over, but designs on the pink marble columns, painted in 1912 by San Antonio artists Ferdinand Stockert and Hermann Kern, and the elaborately carved altar remain as a constant reminder of the past.

Painted Churches

As the Czech and German immigrants to Texas established their homes and communities in the mid to late 1800s, these hard working people brought with them their devout faith in God and strong ties to the architecture of their homelands. The four painted churches of Fayette County in Central Texas, miniature Gothic Revival-style churches with pointed arches and vaulted ceilings, are a living legacy of the area's early pioneers.

The intricately painted designs on the ceilings (and at one time the walls) of the churches at Ammannsville, Dubina, Praha, and High Hill, all located within a few miles of each other, are essentially folk-art interpretations of the European painted churches. Parishioners provided all the labor and craftsmanship and also furnished their beloved tiny structures with all the lavish accouterments of the day—stained glass windows (often ordered from Europe) and elaborately carved altars and statues and columns. "To enter these churches," writes Sophia Dembling, freelancer for the *Dallas Morning News*, "is to step from the spacious simplicity of the Texas landscape into the richness of the Victorian Catholic's vision of the Kingdom of Heaven."

Mission Espiritu Santo Church in Goliad

One tradition special to our family during the holidays is lighting the candles on our home Advent wreath. Each Sunday evening, we light the candle and have a small devotional service as we prepare for the celebration of Jesus' birth.

—LEE WISE, *Brownfield*

MY MOST MEMORABLE TEXAS CHRISTMAS
by Elaine Crane, Kingwood

My family moved to Corpus Christi shortly before Christmas in 1939, and it was only me, my two sisters, and our parents that day to celebrate. After we had opened our gifts, and we girls were playing with some of our toys, someone knocked at the door. It was a homeless man (we called them tramps in those days). He said he was all alone and wondered if he could have a cup of coffee or a sandwich. My dad invited him in and gave him breakfast and coffee. The man told us he had had a family and was now separated from them, and it really meant a lot to see a family like ours enjoying being together. He stayed awhile, and then went on his way. Looking back now, I think of what it must have meant to him, but it also gave us girls an unforgettable look at the true meaning of Christmas.

SALADO UNITED METHODIST CHURCH

This Texas Historic Landmark in the heart of Salado has served the community since 1890 and is often featured on the Homes Tour during the first weekend of Salado's annual Christmas Stroll. It also holds the distinction of being entered in the National Register of Historic Places.

This colorful nativity decorates the grounds of Immaculate Conception Catholic Church in Panna Maria, reputed to be the oldest Polish settlement in the United States.

MISSION SAN JOSÉ, SAN ANTONIO

Mission San José, built in the early 1700s by the Franciscan friars, is considered one of the most magnificent missions in the country because of its classic Spanish Colonial architecture and ornate craftsmanship. One of the highlights of the church year is the annual presentation of the Christmas pageant, Los Pastores.

(right)
Resplendent nativity displays wearing halos of tiny, white lights grace the interior of the beautiful Nativity of the Blessed Virgin Mary Catholic Church in the tiny Polish town of Cestohowa (originally Czestochowa).

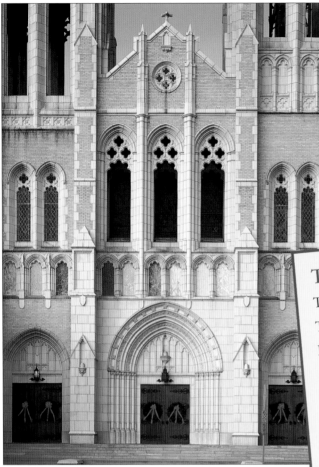

The First Methodist Church in Fort Worth

One December 24th morning, when the weather had been especially cold, wet, and nasty for a week, there was no sign of improvement. My neighbor and I, who had seven cranky, housebound, "How-many-more-hours-'til-Christmas?" young children between us, discovered that we had both experienced a similar Christmas tradition as children—a birthday party for the Baby Jesus. We decided right then and there to revive the tradition for our own children.

That afternoon we let the children dress up in party clothes. Then we started the party by telling a very simplified story of the birth of the Christ Child. A small manger scene served as the centerpiece for the table. We sang "Happy Birthday" to the Baby Jesus, and there was ice cream and a cake with seven candles. Each child got to blow out one candle and the older ones got to proclaim a "birthday gift" to the Child, such as "I'll try to remember to pick up my toys," or "I won't whine at bedtime."

As the years went on, the party grew to include all of the young children on our block, and the older children helped out with decorations, party favors, arranging simple games, leading songs, and storytelling.

— **PAT SCHUMAN**, *Fredericksburg*

THE CANDLE AND THE ROSE

The candle at midnight, the red rose at dawn
The blessings The Father sends us with His Son
Illumination's flaring, the ardent gem glows
Anticipation's flower, the petals of the rose

Enkindle the spirit, emblazon the soul
Awaken the heart to Love's peaceful control
These candles of Advent we light in His Name
Flame rising to flower, flower falling to flame

These candles of Advent we light in His name
Flame rising to flower, flower falling to flame

GEOFF WALKER, *Midland*

Each year on the first Sunday of Advent, St. Laurence Catholic Church of Sugar Land launches its "Wish Upon a Star" program. Three large trees are totally covered with nearly 2,000 paper stars defining needs of others from across the city. Each colored star signifies an organization that needs help at holiday time. This year help will be going to two schools in Columbia staffed by the Basilian Fathers, and Catholic Charities Elderly Services.

A committee of twelve makes the stars, decorates the trees, and sees that the packages are delivered near Christmas. What a wonderful sight to see the generosity of the parishioners when the stars are returned to the church in the middle of December on top of packages wrapped and ready to deliver.

— **ANN BUCHMANN**, *Sugar Land*

The original Chappell Hill United Methodist Church
was built on this site in 1853, but was destroyed by the great
hurricane of 1900. The present building was erected in 1901
and is now listed as a Texas Historic Landmark.

SAN ELIZARIO MISSION
southeast of El Paso

The figure of Christ rises majestically over the
decorated altar at San Elizario Mission. The church
is estimated to have been built in 1843, but
the mission itself dates back to the late 1680s.

BIRTH, REBIRTH

Each time a child is born, Christ comes again.
With each soul's venturing, His birth takes place.
"Even as you have done it unto the least of these,
You have done it unto me."

Each time a mother brings a child into the world
Christ is again among us
Telling us — "this will you do and more also
Because I go to the Father."

With each sun's rising, He brings us hope
Through those who intersect our lives.
With each encounter we meet Him,
Love Him, and are blest by Him.

Every day is Christmas!
Every moment Resurrection!
Be born! Live!
For thus, Joy grows.
Thus, Light continues.

JANE CLANCY DEBENPORT, *Temple*

*San Elizario Presidio Chapel,
San Elizario (near El Paso)*

88

Hanukkah

As the sun sets on the twenty-fifth day of Kislev on the Hebrew lunar calendar, Jewish families all across Texas begin the joyous celebration of Hanukkah by lighting the first candle of the nine-branched menorah, called a hanukkiah. Each of the eight days of this Festival of Lights, the shamash (helper candle) is used to light another candle until all eight candles are shining as a testimony to the ancient miracle of burning oil.

Today the same faith that gave the ancient Hebrew people the courage to light the single vessel of oil, barely enough for one day, which burned in the Temple for eight days after the triumphant defeat of Antiochus in 165 B.C.E., gives modern Jewish families the same strength to teach their children the importance of tradition and spirituality. One San Antonio rabbi was quoted as saying, "To me, the Hanukkah candles tell us that everything is possible. In San Antonio, circa 1998, it's possible to live as a Jew, to practice as a Jew, to observe as a Jew, to worship as a Jew." Since Hanukkah usually falls within the Christmas season, the challenge, especially in areas where there are few Jewish people, is to keep the Jewish traditions glowing along with the candles.

As with most Jewish holidays, the Hanukkah traditions and festivities center around the family and gatherings where special foods, like Sufganiyot (jelly doughnuts) or Potato Latkes (potato pancakes), play an important role because they are fried in oil, a reminder of the miracle of the first Hanukkah. Because of Jewish dietary restrictions that forbid serving dairy and meat at the same meal, applesauce instead of sour cream is used as a garnish for the latkes if the main course contains meat (which in Texas could sometimes even be chili!).

POTATO LATKES

4 large potatoes
1 small onion
2 eggs, beaten
2–4 Tbsp. flour
1 tsp. salt
¼ tsp. white pepper
frying oil
applesauce or sour cream

Peel potatoes and onion. Grate potatoes and onion coarsely, then mix with eggs, 2 Tbsp. flour (adding rest of flour if needed to make right texture) and seasonings. Heat oil (½ inch deep) in nonstick frying pan. Drop large spoonfuls of mixture into the hot oil. Fry, turning once, to a golden brown. Serve with either applesauce or sour cream.

From the large menorah on the square outside Houston City Hall to the tiniest child-crafted replica, Jewish Texans light their candles and thank God for the miracles of the past and the blessings of being able to celebrate freely. One inspired South Texas rabbi said, "As each candle on the menorah is lit during Hanukkah, so also should a believer's inner light grow and spread in life. The fact that every night we add a light also teaches us that we should never be satisfied with today's light."

𝒦wanzaa

DECEMBER 26–JANUARY 1

In 1966, Dr. Maulana Karenga created the new American holiday called "Kwanzaa" as a time for African-Americans to celebrate their African history and culture. This joyous new holiday is loosely based on African harvest festivals, from which comes the Swahili phrase *Matunda Ya Kwanza* (meaning "first fruits"). Dr. Karenga added the extra "a" to Kwanza (meaning "first") to distinguish the African-American from the African since this is a holiday celebrated only in America.

All around Texas, especially in the larger cities, African Americans gather in community centers and homes to celebrate the seven days of Kwanzaa. Each year, for example, Houston's Texas Southern University holds a ceremony for children and representatives of the African American community to begin this week-long festival of learning and dedication. As the first candle in the *kinarah* (kee-nah-rah) is lit, there is a sense of unity with other African Americans around the state and the country as well as a connection to their African heritage.

The number seven plays an important role in the festivities as there are seven symbols on the table, seven candles, called *mishumaa saba* (mee-shu-mah sah-bah), in the kinarah, and seven principles, called *nguzo saba* (en-goo-zoh sah-bah). Each day a candle representing one of the principles is lit, beginning with the center black candle and alternating between the red and green candles on succeeding days. The day begins with the greeting, *"Habari gani?" ("What is the news?")* which is answered with the principle to be celebrated that day.

DAY 1

Umoja (oo-moh-jah)
The first principle means *unity* in family, community, nation, and race.

DAY 2

Kujichagulia (koo-jee-cha-goo-lee-yah)
The second principle means *self-determination.*
This is a day to learn to identify with the African-American culture and define identities for themselves.

DAY 3

Ujima (oo-jee-mah)

The third principle is *responsibility and working together* to make a stronger community.

DAY 4

Ujamaa (oo-jah-mah)

The fourth principle means *cooperative economics*—establishing businesses and buying from each other.

This colorful festival, full of singing, dancing, feasting, story-telling and creative arts, celebrates and embraces the rich heritage of the past while offering renewed strength for the future.

DAY 5

Nia (nee-yah)

The fifth principle means *purpose*. This is a day to contemplate actions and consequences as well as dream about future accomplishments.

DAY 6

Kuumba (koo-oom-bah)

The sixth principle means *creativity* and encourages people to use all of their talents to think of better ways to do things in any walk of life.

DAY 7

Imani (ee-mah-nee)

The seventh principle means *faith*—believing in themselves, their parents, their teachers, and their race. The other six principles of Kwanzaa are empty without this faith.

CHEF DAVE'S WARM SALAD

of field greens, goat cheese, and port-soaked cherries in pancetta vinaigrette

Salad ingredients:
1 ½ lb. field greens, Mescalune mix
1 6 oz. log goat cheese, crumbled
½ cup port-soaked Cherries
(use sun-dried cherries)
½ cup port wine

Pancetta vinaigrette ingredients:
¼ lb. pancetta
½ cup sherry vinegar
¾ cup olive oil
10 shallots, sliced
½ Tbsp. garlic, minced
¼ cup pancetta drippings
1 Tbsp. thyme, fresh, chopped
Salt and finely ground black pepper,
to taste

To make salad, wash and dry greens; reserve. Crumble goat cheese and reserve. Heat port to a simmer and pour over sun-dried cherries and reserve.

To make pancetta, render pancetta until golden brown and crisp; strain and reserve both drippings and pancetta. Lightly sauté shallots and garlic until aromatic.

In a large bowl whisk together sherry vinegar, olive oil, shallots, garlic and drippings, and thyme, season to taste.

To assemble salad in a bowl, heat port-soaked cherries and crumbled goat cheese (I heat it in a 350° F oven). Then, add greens and warm slightly. Remove from heat and toss with warm vinaigrette dressing and serve on individual plates. Serves 10.

—**Dave Hermann**, *The Range at the Barton House, Salado*

This delectable Warm Salad recipe from Chef Dave Hermann and his wife Katie, both graduates of the Culinary Institute of America, is just one of the mouth-watering specialties at The Range at the Barton House, *located in the heart of historic Salado. The Barton House, a Texas historic landmark that the Hermanns restored, was built in 1866 for Dr. Wellborn Barton, a pioneer physician of the region.*

—**Dave and Katie Hermann**

SPINACH MADELEINE

2 packages frozen chopped spinach
4 Tbsp. butter
2 Tbsp. flour
2 Tbsp. chopped onion
½ cup evaporated milk
½ cup spinach liquid

¾ tsp. celery salt
¾ tsp. garlic salt
salt to taste
6 oz. Jalepeno cheddar cheese
1 tsp. Worcestershire sauce
½ tsp. black pepper

Cook spinach according to package directions. Drain and reserve the liquid.

Melt butter in pan over low heat. Add flour, stirring until blended and smooth, but not brown. Add liquid slowly, stirring constantly to avoid lumps. Cook until smooth and thick; continue stirring. Add seasonings and cheese, which has been cut into small pieces. Stir until melted. Combine with cooked spinach. This may be served immediately or put into a casserole dish and topped with buttered bread crumbs.

Bake at 350° F for 25 minutes or until bubbling. This dish may be made the day before and then baked. It may also be frozen. Serves 5–6.

—**Mary Ware Knudsen**, *Sugar Land*

This is a favorite side dish from the Cajun side of my family. It is a staple for the holidays at our house.

—**Mary Ware Knudsen**

Opposite: A country-style Christmas turkey dinner
Overleaf: Enchanted Rock State Natural Area

This is a great salad for holidays!

—LANNA KUEHL

I grew up on a farm in East Texas, and Christmas was one of the most exciting times of the year. On Christmas Eve when all the families had gathered, we started off the evening with fireworks and sparklers; that was always the favorite with us kids! Then everyone sat around and told stories—my uncle kept us all on the edge of our seats with tales of the years gone by. Sometimes we told Bible stories, but mostly it was a time to reflect on the year past and to be together. On Christmas morning, we got baskets with nuts, candy, and the best-tasting apples in the world. Round about one o'clock in the afternoon, we'd have the biggest meal of the year—ham, turkey, fried chicken, and ALL the fixings. Of course, before we could eat, there was always a prayer—I can remember, as a boy, thinking that the prayer would last F O R E V E R— they had to thank God for every leaf on every tree and bless every drop of rain that had fallen that year— and with all that food in front of me smelling sooooo good, all I wanted to do was EAT.

—NATHAN FARR, *Houston*

MOGEN DAVID SALAD

2 packages black cherry Jello
2 cups hot water
1 cup Mogen David wine
2 cans dark, sweet pitted cherries
1 cup cherry juice
 (drained from cherries above)

Topping
½ pint sour cream
20 large marshmallows, cut up

Make both Jello and topping the day before serving.

Dissolve Jello in hot water; add wine and cherry juice. Let sit until partially set, then add cherries and pour into mold or 9" by 13" glass dish and chill.

To make topping, cut up marshmallows and stir into sour cream and refrigerate overnight.

Right before serving, whip marshmallow mixture and pour over unmolded salad. (When I use the 9" by 13" pan, I leave it in the pan, put sour cream mixture on top, and cut into squares to serve.)

—LANNA KUEHL, *Houston*

CALICO CORN SALAD

2 11 oz. cans whole kernel corn
⅓ cup Chablis or other white wine
¼ cup chopped green pepper
½ cup chopped purple onion
1 4 oz. jar diced pimento
2 Tbsp. chopped fresh cilantro

2 Tbsp. rice wine vinegar
2 tsp. lime juice
¼ tsp. salt
¼ tsp. garlic powder
¼ tsp. ground red pepper
lettuce leaves (optional)

Combine corn and wine in large nonstick skillet; place over medium heat and cook 3 to 5 minutes or until liquid evaporates. Remove from heat and add green pepper and next 8 ingredients, stirring well. Chill.

To serve, spoon corn mixture into lettuce-lined bowl.

Yields 8 (½-cup) servings

—CASSIE SULLIVAN, *Cat Spring*

FESTIVE FRUIT SALAD

1 20 oz. can pineapple chunks
 packed in juice
1 20 oz. can pears, drained and chopped
3 kiwi fruit, peeled and sliced
2 chopped, unpeeled apples

2 11 oz. cans mandarin oranges, drained
1 cup pecan halves
3 Tbsp. all-purpose flour
½ cup sugar
1 egg, lightly beaten

Drain pineapple, reserving juice. Set pineapple aside. Pour juice into a small saucepan; add sugar and flour. Bring to a boil. Quickly stir in egg; cook until thickened. Remove from heat; cool. Refrigerate. In a large bowl, combine pineapple, oranges, pears, kiwi, apples, and pecans. Pour dressing over and blend well. Cover and chill for 1 hour. Yields 12–16 servings.

—PANSY D. BENEDICT, *Fredricksburg*

Party fare with spicy Texas flare

GALVESTON CRAB CAKES

1 lb. fresh lump crabmeat

¾ cup Italian breadcrumbs

1 large egg, beaten

¼ cup mayonnaise

1 tsp. Worcestershire sauce

1 tsp. dry mustard

½ tsp. salt

¼ tsp. black pepper

½ tsp. parsley

oil for frying

lemon wedges

Place crabmeat in large bowl and, without breaking up the lumps too much, carefully remove cartilage and shell. Add breadcrumbs and mix gently. In a separate bowl, combine egg, mayonnaise, Worcestershire sauce, mustard, salt, pepper, and parsley. Gently blend with crabmeat mixture. Form mixture into 6 patties. In a large skillet, fry the cakes in oil until golden brown—about 3 minutes on each side. Serve with lemon wedges. May be made ahead of time and reheated. May also be frozen.

—**MARY WARE KNUDSEN,** *Sugar Land*

A memorable, but not traditional, Christmas meal occurred the year both my son, Bill, and I were tired of turkey and trimmings; so, aided by the unseasonably warm weather, he grilled T-bone steaks over mesquite charcoal on the patio, supplemented by twice-baked potatoes, garlic toast, and a huge tossed salad.

—**LOUISE CROCKER,** *Midland*

97

PINEAPPLE BUTTERMILK SALAD

1 16-oz. can crushed pineapple, undrained
2 Tbsp. sugar (optional)
1 6-oz. package orange-flavored gelatin
2 cups buttermilk

1 8-oz. package frozen whipped topping, thawed
1 cup chopped pecans (optional)

Combine pineapple and sugar in saucepan. Bring to boil, stirring occasionally. Remove from heat. Add gelatin, stirring until dissolved. Cool. Add buttermilk and stir until combined. Fold in whipped topping and pecans. Spoon into 12" by 8" or 13" by 9" inch dish. Sprinkle with pecans. Chill about 2 hours.

Yields 8–10 servings.

—ALINE PARKS, *Snyder*

BUTTERMILK PECAN CHICKEN

⅓ cup butter or margarine
1 cup all-purpose flour
1 cup pecans, ground
¼ cup sesame seeds
1 Tbsp. paprika
1½ tsp. salt

⅛ tsp. pepper
1 egg, slightly beaten
1 cup buttermilk
8 chicken breast halves, skinned and boned
¼ cup pecans, coarsely chopped

Melt butter in a 13" by 9" by 2" inch dish; set aside. Combine flour, ground pecans, sesame seeds, paprika, salt, and pepper. Combine egg and buttermilk. Dip chicken in egg mixture, and dredge in flour mixture, coating thoroughly. Place in baking dish, turning once to coat with butter. Sprinkle with pecans. Bake chicken at 350° F for 30 minutes or until done. Makes 8 servings.

—MARJORIE OTTE, *Stonewall*

TURKEY SOPA

Leftover turkey, cut in bite-sized pieces
1 dozen corn tortillas
2 chopped onions
1 lb. grated Monterey Jack cheese

1 can cream of chicken soup
2 cans Rotel tomatoes and green chilies
sour cream—optional

In glass rectangular baking dish, tear each tortilla into 8 pieces. Line bottom of dish with tortilla pieces, overlapping. Set aside.

In big skillet, sauté onions, then pour in soup and Rotel tomatoes and chilies. Stir and simmer on low for 10 minutes.

Spread turkey pieces over tortillas, scooping up enough onion mixture to cover turkey. Sprinkle cheese generously over first layer. Repeat layers until dish is full. Sprinkle more cheese on last layer. (Optional—cover casserole with sour cream.)

Cover casserole with aluminum foil and bake at 350° F for 45 minutes.

—CAROLYN TUCKER, *El Paso*

CORNBREAD DRESSING

Crumbled cornbread (about 4 cups)	1 cup finely chopped celery
Day old bread, torn in pieces (about 4 cups)	2 Tbsp. butter (or as desired)
2 eggs, slightly beaten	giblets, cooked and finely chopped
salt and pepper to taste	broth from giblets
1 cup finely chopped onion	chopped parsley (optional)
	pinch of sage (optional)

Put bread and cornbread in bowl. Add eggs, salt, pepper, onion, celery, butter, and giblets, which have been cooked in water and chopped. Add enough broth the giblets were cooked in to make stuffing the texture desired. (If cooked separately, mixture should be very moist.)

Dressing can be baked in the turkey or baked in a separate pan at 350° F for 1 hour.

—**DOROTHY BUJNOCH,** *Hallettsville*

No Texas holiday book would be complete without Cornbread Dressing, and people in Hallettsville consider this THE ultimate recipe!

—**PAT CARR,** *Hallettsville*

Antler tree at the King Ranch Saddle Shop

RICE DRESSING

1 stick margarine	4 cups water
8 Tbsp. slivered almonds	4 chicken bouillon cubes
8 Tbsp. finely chopped onions	4 tsp. lemon juice
	1½ tsp. salt
1⅓ cups uncooked long-grain rice	8 oz. chopped mushrooms (canned or fresh)

In saucepan, melt butter and cook almonds, onion, and rice in the butter for 5–10 minutes, stirring frequently. Add water, bouillon cubes, lemon juice, and salt. Bring mixture to boil, stirring to dissolve cubes. Reduce heat, cover, and cook slowly—about 20–25 minutes or until liquid is absorbed and rice is fluffy. Stir in drained mushrooms.

—**ANN BUCHMANN,** *Sugar Land*

This is one of the first recipes I learned to cook, and it has been on our holiday tables ever since.

—**ANN BUCHMANN**

For me, Christmas means having all 15 members of my family together. Our Christmas meal comes mostly from the bounty of my garden and farm: venison roast, turkey and dressing, homemade sausage and ham. We also use cedar from our farm to decorate and fill the house with that wonderful, homey Christmas scent.

—**MILDRED O. JENSCHKE,** *Stonewall*

HOLIDAY SWEET POTATO CASSEROLE

4 cups mashed sweet potatoes	½ tsp. nutmeg	½ cup nuts
1 stick oleo	½ tsp. vanilla	½ stick margarine
1 cup evaporated milk	*Topping*	½ cup brown sugar
1 cup sugar	1 cup crushed corn flakes	
2 eggs	(takes about 2–3 cups	
¾ tsp. cinnamon	regular flakes)	

Beat potatoes with melted oleo and add remaining ingredients, except topping. Bake in oven in 9" by 13" inch casserole dish for 15 minutes at 425° F. Remove, add topping, and bake additional 15 minutes at 400° F. Serves 15.

For topping, mix all topping ingredients together and spread over sweet potato mixture.

—**JEWELL RATZLAFF,** *Perryton*

I served Holiday Sweet Potato Casserole on Christmas Day and even my neighbor, who doesn't like sweet potatoes, had two extra servings!

—**ELLEN EARLE,** *Sugar Land*

Our traditional Christmas dinner is barbecued brisket, ribs, and all the trimmings!

—DOUG BEICH, *Grand Prairie*

Edgewood Heritage Park Historical Village is the focal point of downtown Edgewood and is the site for many community celebrations. Founded in 1976 as a bicentennial ongoing project, this outdoor museum's purpose is to preserve the rural culture and architectural heritage of Texas for present and future generations. Since Van Zandt County is famous for its sweet potatoes, Edgewood Heritage Park always serves these little muffins when groups tour the museum.

History comes alive at Christmas Along the Corridor in Goliad

SWEET POTATO MUFFINS

1 ½ cups flour
½ cup raisins
1 ¼ cups sugar
½ cup pecans
2 tsp. baking powder
1 cup milk
½ cup melted butter

1 tsp. cinnamon
2 beaten eggs
¼ tsp. salt
1 ¼ cup mashed sweet potatoes
½ tsp. ground cloves
¼ tsp. vanilla

Mix dry ingredients; add remaining ingredients and stir with spoon. Batter will be lumpy. Bake in mini muffin pan that has been sprayed with Pam about 15–17 minutes at 400° F.

— EDGEWOOD HERITAGE PARK, *Edgewood*

"BRONCO" BREAD/MUFFINS

2 Tbsps. butter, softened

¼ cup HOT water

½ cup orange juice

1½ Tbsp. grated orange rind

1 egg

1 cup blueberries

1 cup sugar

2 cups flour

1 tsp. baking powder

½ tsp. salt

¼ tsp. baking soda

Combine butter, water, orange juice, and orange rind in a bowl. Add egg and mix well. Mix in all dry ingredients. Last, fold in blueberries by hand so as not to crush them.

Bake at 350° F in greased 9" by 5" pan for about 70 minutes, or make into muffins and bake 30 to 40 minutes depending on the size of the muffin tin used.

—ELLEN EARLE, *Sugar Land*

I make these every Christmas morning because they're so easy and the whole house smells so good. We do our stockings while we wait for a hot muffin!

—ELLEN EARLE

GWENSKE ROLLS

⅔ cup finely chopped pecans

⅓ cup brown sugar

⅓ cup confectioners sugar

1 tsp. cinnamon

¼ cup butter, softened

2 loaves frozen white bread dough, thawed

Topping

1 cup confectioners sugar

1 Tbsp. butter, melted

2 to 3 Tbsp. cream

In a small bowl combine the first 5 ingredients. Roll dough out on a lightly floured surface to a small rectangle. Spread with the nut mixture. Roll up lengthwise and cut into 1-inch rolls. Place the rolls in a greased pan. Cover with soft cloth and place on top of stove that is preheating to 375° F. Let rise for 1 to 1½ hours. When rolls are fully risen, carefully place in oven and bake for 10 minutes or until lightly brown. Combine the topping ingredients and drizzle over the warm rolls. Makes about 14 to 16 rolls.

—GWEN AND DAVID FULLBROOK, *Innkeepers
Camp David, a traditional bed & breakfast in Fredericksburg*

Our favorite family holiday tradition is gathering the whole family together for Christmas Eve dinner—-turkey with cornbread stuffing, both mashed and sweet potatoes, onions, brussel sprouts, cranberry molded salad, and mince meat pies—it's WONDERFUL!

—BETTY HIGGINS, *Llano*

MEXICAN BLACK-EYED PEAS

1 lb. dried black-eyed peas

2 lb. bulk pork sausage

1 medium onion, chopped

1 (18 oz.) can whole tomatoes, undrained

½ cup water

2 Tbsp. sugar

2½ Tbsp. chili powder

2 tsp. garlic salt

¼ tsp. black pepper

2½ Tbsp. chopped celery

Wash and sort peas; cover with 2 inches water and soak overnight.

Next day, brown sausage; add onion and cook until tender; drain.

Drain peas and stir in sausage, onion, and rest of ingredients. Bring to a boil. Cover and simmer 1½ to 2 hours until tender. Add hot water, if needed. (Hot peppers may be added, too!)

—MARY LOU FULLER, *San Angelo*

This is a favorite at all our family reunions, holidays, and get-togethers—sometimes there are over a hundred of us! We just love to get together and cook the traditional family recipes that have been handed down to us from our mothers and grandmothers.

—MARY LOU FULLER

Kris Kringle (Swiss), Swarte Piet (Dutch), and St Nicholas (Asia Minor) at the Santa Claus Museum in Columbus

The Mary Elizabeth Hopkins Santa Claus Museum

COLUMBUS, TEXAS

The 2,000-plus Santas who live in this delightful, year-round museum could convince even that long-ago, young Virginia that Santa Claus really does exist. In 1990, when Mary Elizabeth Hopkins died, the Hopkins family and Magnolia Homes Tour, Inc., created this museum to house this vast collection of Mary Elizabeth's "toys," as her husband lovingly referred to them, so that children of all ages could enjoy the spirit of Christmas any time of the year.

Mary Elizabeth collected Santas of every imaginable shape and size, made out of everything from papier mâché to wood, from tin to lace, gourds to corn shucks. She also created needlework Santas on pillows, pictures, and ornaments. After a while, family and friends got into the "spirit" and brought Santas to her from around the world. All of these treasures fill display case after display case, evoking wistful memories of Christmas past for "oldsters" and gleeful hopes of Christmas future for "youngsters."

From above the beautiful, 1860s Hopkins home mantelpiece, Mary Elizabeth's portrait overlooks a family parlor setting decorated for her favorite season. A Christmas tree in full Santa regalia, twinkling with Santa lights (of course), graces the right side of the mantel opposite a jolly, life-sized Santa who stands ready to greet visitors both young and old.

So many Santas—music boxes, toys, cookie jars, needlework, ornaments, postcards, banks, Coca-Cola Santas, Duncan Royale Santas, Neiman Marcus and even Walmart Santas—all beloved by Mary Elizabeth Hopkins, and now shared with the world.

The star of our family decorations was a plywood Santa that Dad had constructed in the garage. You could see Santa high on the rooftop from six blocks away, waving to gawking carloads of children and parents. One particularly blustery West Texas Christmas, Kris Kringle's anchor lines snapped and he went sailing off into the night, completely forgetting his sleigh. Fortunately, the neighborhood search party found Santa two days later in a vacant lot halfway across town.

—GEOFF WALKER, *Midland*

Museum Parlor decorated for Mary Elizabeth's favorite season

My Christmas Surprise
by Lola Woods, Gonzales

I grew up in the tiny farming community of Harwood, near Gonzales, and I remember the year I was six all I wanted for Christmas was a calf. I had heart surgery right before Christmas that year, and I remember everyone was real worried about me. But by Christmas Eve they let me go out in the pasture to see the calves and help feed them. I looked at all the calves and found just the one I wanted and told Granddad, "I want that one right there." They all laughed and took me up to the house. That night, Grandma put on a record of Little Jimmy Dickens singin' "Bessie the Heifer," and I sang with that record all the rest of the night:

> *My daddy gave a calf to me*
> *For a Christmas present once.*
> *I picked a little heifer out,*
> *'Cuz both of us was runts!*

Next morning when everybody came down to open Christmas presents, there was my present standing right by the tree—MY little calf with a big red bow tied around its neck. I never forgot that Christmas or that song.

Every December, when we bring in boxes containing Christmas decorations, we set an annual ritual in motion. At age fifteen, Munchkin, the oldest of our five fur-children (pound puppies), singles out the box containing her stocking as quickly as if she could read the spelling of her name. With tail a-wagging, she then supervises its hanging. She excitedly checks the empty stocking several times each day until Santa fills it on Christmas Eve, then guards it carefully, refusing to budge until she receives its contents the next morning.

Each of our current four-legged children has its own stocking to "open" Christmas morning. Little ones who have passed on to their heavenly home are each lovingly remembered at our house with their own named stockings containing little angel-puppies inside.

What a pleasure it is to watch their little faces light up as we give them their toys and treats from Santa. They give us so very much more in return.

—**Charles & Debbie Smithdeal**, *Fredericksburg*

The children's bedroom at Thistle Hill in Fort Worth

GIFT-GIVING FUN

by Genlyn Anderson, Seminole

With twenty-five people in our family, we had to come up with a different and fun gift-giving tradition. Each person buys one gift (we set a $25 limit) and wraps it. We pile all the gifts in the middle of the floor, and then everyone pulls a number from a jar. #1 picks a gift from the pile and unwraps it—it's always fun to see whether a person goes for the biggest present or not! Then #2 can either take #1's gift or choose another wrapped present. And on it goes with each number—with the rule that a present can only change hands three times. Every year there is at least one thing that everybody fights over. One year all the guys were fighting to get a rod and reel. Another year people were trading like crazy for the seven tea towels I had hand-embroidered—one for each day of the week. The first one who opened the towels was a cook and really wanted to keep them, so he hid them behind his back. When someone came to him and wanted the towels, he gave them just two, but that didn't fool anybody!!! Christmas in our family is NEVER dull!

MOO---OINK! MERRY CHRISTMAS
by Lane Hutchins, Fredericksburg

A select Fredericksburg ladies' group known as the Company of Women (COW) has a Christmas party each year, highlighted by a "Chinese gift-exchange." Each member brings a gift, wrapped and unlabeled. Later, members draw numbers, then each selects one of the gifts in order of numbers drawn, from low to high. When each gift is unwrapped (also in order), the member holding the next highest number has the option of "taking" that gift in exchange for her unopened package. Each higher number has the same option, so a particularly desirable gift may change hands several times.

One year, when an unusual-looking hat box was opened, something black and squealing leapt from the box and frantically darted around the room full of shrieking women attired in fine velvet dresses. When the creature finally slowed, it was identified as a baby, pot-bellied pig.

The energized piglet was subdued only after near mayhem among magnificent Christmas decorations. Alas—tradition prevailed, however; and the hairy little critter was wrested from the lace jabot of its temporary owner by the holder of the next-highest number. This process repeated over and over, with each woman present coveting the adorable little pig, until a verbal fight broke out among several members. In an act of desperation to end the melee, the horrified hostess eventually shooed everybody out the door.

Almost nobody remembers who finally went home with the pig. But nobody has forgotten the occasion. Each December in Fredericksburg, this incident is still recalled, and laughed about as that time a pig broke up the COW's Christmas party.

NEIGHBORHOOD SANTA
by Dottie Priger, Houston

Despite all the last-minute chores Santa has to do, he still finds time to stop at the homes of our neighborhood youngsters for a personal visit. Those visits are a favorite memory of our now grown children. They wondered for years how Santa always knew their good deeds, teachers' names, favorite foods, and so on.

In early December there are lots of whispers and phone calls in our Memorial Bend subdivision as our civic association volunteers gather "inside" information and organize Santa's schedule.

On the appointed day, three dads—"reindeer"—transport the big guy, so they can trade off and be at home at the right time. No one enjoyed it more than my husband, Blitzen!

For 20 or 25 years, we have been part of a "tradition" for a unique Christmas Eve Santa Claus party begun by friends in West University long before they had grandchildren. They invite about 100 young children and their parents (and other friends) to gather at their house about 3:00 p.m. Christmas Eve to meet Santa Claus. People begin gathering about 2:30 and eagerly await Santa's arrival. How he will arrive is a closely held secret, but promptly at the appointed hour Santa's parade can be spotted at the end of their street. Amid cheers and glee, he approaches in a fire truck, in a sleigh (on wheels) drawn by "Chinese reindeer," in a "high Rider," or maybe on horseback— every year they dream up a different conveyance.

Once there, Santa mounts his throne and takes each child on his lap to hear his heart's desires as photos are taken and favors dispersed—one year the favors were clear balls with goldfish inside! The crowd then mills through the house and the back garden to visit, eat from the lavish buffet, and enjoy singing Christmas carols and whatever other entertainment is provided —one year an ice sculptor carved an almost life-sized Santa Claus during the course of the party.

This festivity has become a major celebration of the season for many of us, and it has never been canceled because of inclement weather. I can remember only one year when it was truly nasty—I really thought the house would never recover from the inch or two of mud that was tracked through it! We often leave town for Christmas, but we never leave before Christmas Eve if we can help it.

—JINNY BARNHART, Houston

105

One of my most memorable Christmases was the year my son Bill's special gift was to take me to a performance of Handel's Messiah *by the Dallas Bach Society.*

—LOUISE CROCKER, *Midland*

CHRISTMAS ON ZOOGUS

Zoogus is a planet that you won't find
For it is hidden in my mind.
We have Christmas everywhere
We don't have trees and stuff
We just have a big, big fluff.
We don't have those candy canes
We just have candy lanes!

— ANDY WILDS *(age 8), Temple*

When I was a child, we often spent Christmas with grandparents, aunts, uncles, and cousins all under one roof. We had a tradition that each person wrapped all the gifts they were giving to others in the same wrapping paper. For instance, one aunt would use green paper with white ribbon, Grammom used red and white striped paper, someone else used snowflakes, poinsettias, or Christmas tree paper.

On Christmas Eve, one by one, we opened our gifts from each other. Even though we sometimes stayed up late, the children's "Santa" presents were always under the tree when the first little one woke up on Christmas morning!

The sled, bicycle, dollhouse, and other special presents from Santa were never wrapped, of course, but occasionally, for something small enough for a gift box, Santa always wrapped with Santa paper!

—PAT SCHUMAN, *Fredericksburg*

I buy each of my eight dogs new "special" collars for the holidays! Even my cat of one year received hers this year!

—SUSAN WILLIAMS, *Decatur*

Concho River Lights, San Angelo

Santa Claus is Coming, Children

1. San -ta Claus is com - ing, child -ren, He'll be here in one day.
2. Hark, I think I hear him com - ing. He's climb-ing on the roof.

He is ve - ry anx - ious, child -ren, to come when you're a - way.
Though the snow lies deep up on it, I can hear each rain - deer's hoof.

So - - Hang up your stock - ings and go to bed quick- ly, and
So - - Hang up your stock - ings and go to bed quick- ly, and

close your eyes tight as you can - - - - - - - - - -, for he'll
close yurr eyes tight as you can - - -- - - - - - -, for he'll

peep through the key - hole to see if you're sleep - ing, that
peep through the key - hole to see if you're sleep - ing, that

good- na - tured jol - ly old man - - - - - .
good- na - tured jol - ly old man - - - - - .

CHORUS:

SO—hang up your stockings *(reach up as if to a nail stuck in the mantel)*

And go to bed quickly *(hands palm to palm at the side of a cheek like a pillow)*

And close your eyes tight as you can. *(squeeze eyes shut)*

For he'll peek through the keyhole to see if you're sleeping,

   (eye peeking through circle made by thumb and index finger)

That good-natured, jolly old man! *(shake index finger in time to the words)*

VERSE 2

Hark! I think I hear him coming, *(hand cupped behind ear)*

He's climbing on the roof. *(point upward)*

Though the snow lies deep upon it *(move hand, palm down, back and forth)*

I can hear each reindeer's hoof! *(use hands as hooves making "steps" in the air)*

REPEAT CHORUS

(The second chorus ends with a jolly "Ho-Ho!")

As far back as I can remember, the children in my mother's family have sung "Santa Claus is Coming, Children." As near as I can figure, my mother and her siblings learned this song before 1920, probably at a country school near St. Elmo. We did motions on the chorus and second verse.

—JANE CLANCY DEBENPORT, *Temple*

Texas Santas

Since chances of a snowy Christmas in Texas are slim to none, Santa's sleigh would have a pretty rough haul, and the reindeer would probably call the whole deal off due to "clement" weather! So, when he gets to Texas, Santa (alias Cowboy Kringle, Pancho Claus, or Good Ol' Saint Nick) trades in his sleigh for a fire engine for Round Rock's Brown Santa toy donation or a motorcycle for cruisin' the highways in the Lexington area. He may speed into Corpus Christi aboard a cabin cruiser, and then make the rounds in Goliad aboard a stage coach (pulled by a "Rein-steer," of course!). And no Texas Christmas season would be complete without Cowboy Kringle galloping into historic Gruene, near New Braunfels, to throw the switch on the holiday lights. So come Christmas Eve, the legendary reindeer can lallygag north of the border while Santa continues his annual trek Texas-style atop a buckboard wagon, a horse, a Longhorn steer, or maybe even a helicopter—after all, it is a BIG state!

Santa climbs a rock drill in San Antonio

Greetings from Gruene's Cowboy Kringle

No snow in the forecast? No problem for Lone Star Santas who "wheel" across the state in everything from wagons to motorcycles!

Spec-**DAZZ**-ular!!!!!

What else could we do but make up a new word to describe the billions of Christmas lights emblazoning Texas from border to border. From Marshall's "Wonderland of Lights" to the Hill Country courthouses to Lubbock's "Carol of Lights," Texans put on a holiday "light" show that rivals all the stars in the galaxy.

The Courtland Museum in Marshall

From Thanksgiving to Christmas, the breathtaking array of over seven million tiny, white lights from MARSHALL'S "WONDERLAND OF LIGHTS" sets the East Texas sky aglow. Just as those long-ago shepherds and Magi were led by the magnificent Star of the East, people all over Texas and surrounding states are drawn to bask in the glow of Marshall's "splendificent" display of lights. That magic moment at the official lighting ceremony, when all seven million lights are illuminated, signals the start of an enchanting six-week festival of Christmas lights, candlelight home tours, parades, and music. Nightly tours wend through the dazzling streets of historic downtown past Marshall's shimmering centerpiece, historic Harrison County Courthouse. One resident admits she goes back night after night just to feel that childlike awe inspired by the lighted courthouse. For over a decade the people of Marshall have united to offer this ever changing kaleidoscope of Christmas splendor. It is no wonder that brochures simply proclaim, "Wonderland of Lights . . . where the memories never fade!"

The Zilker Park tree in Austin

Gleaming high above the trees of AUSTIN'S ZILKER PARK stands the 165-foot "Tree of Lights," crown jewel of the month-long Yulefest celebration. Made up of thirty-nine streamers of lights strung from one of Austin's historic moonlight towers, the "Tree of Lights" continues a tradition begun in 1965. Probably the most popular part of this Austin tradition includes walking underneath the tree, grabbing the hands of family and friends, and spinning round and round while looking up to the canopy of lights overhead.

The fun and fellowship continues just down the street from the "Tree of Lights" as holiday revelers enter the magical "Trail of Lights." This mile-long display of festive Christmas and wintertime scenes, interspersed with food booths and entertainment, offers something to tickle the imagination of young and old alike as they stroll along the paths carrying "glow sticks" and perhaps sipping hot chocolate (or ice tea, depending on the weather!) while they enjoy the panorama of sparkling holiday scenes.

A "must see" at Christmas is HALLETTSVILLE'S HISTORIC LAVACA COUNTY COURTHOUSE bathed in the magical glow of over 350,000 lights.

OUR LONGHORN CHRISTMAS
by Joe and Eloise Pantalone, Sweeny

My husband, a former coach, and I are personal friends of the legendary Texas football coach Darrell Royal and his wife. We even named our youngest son Darrell Royal! At Christmas we decorate our white Christmas tree with white lights and trim it entirely with orange for the University of Texas. There are orange bows, orange store-bought ornaments, orange Longhorns, and orange ornaments in the shape of Texas with family members' names on them (even the pets have their own ornaments).

Continuing the orange and white theme, our whole family pitches in at Thanksgiving and decorates the outside of the house. The game room and garage are done in all orange lights and we have the outline of a Longhorn on the roof of the game room and a University of Texas sign on the garage. Not only do we decorate our home for the pleasure it brings our own family, but also for the many townspeople who express to us the pleasure it brings to them and their loved ones during the holiday season. Along about the first of December, the townspeople start asking when we are going to turn on the lights.

DECK THE HALLS

CORPUS CHRISTI, "the Sparkling City by the Sea," really does more than just sparkle every December. The city lights up the harbor sky with a dazzling array of twinkling white lights along the shoreline and the causeway; then it fills the harbor with a flotilla of bejeweled boats for "The Annual Harbor Lights Festival" the first weekend in December. The festival kicks off with an afternoon Children's Parade;

then in the evening, Santa's motorcade moves along Shoreline signaling the lighting of the magnificent 75-foot Tree of Lights, followed, of course, by a fireworks spectacular over the bayfront. What a way to start the holiday season!

When we decorate for the holidays, we put a stuffed Santa with a straw hat and overalls in our old farm wagon, and reindeer with green garland reins that Santa holds. We put chasing lights on the wheels, which makes them appear to be moving.

—**CLARICE HANSTROM,** *Hutto*

In Galena Park we use luminarias placed along the curbs to help convey our special feelings during the holiday season. Friends and neighbors gather for block parties and hayrides, and local churches go caroling.

—**GWEN DI STEFANO,** *Galena Park*

Magic in Marble Falls

Reflected in the waters of LBJ Lake, the MARBLE FALLS "WALKWAY OF LIGHTS" bedazzles its visitors with over a million lights in one hundred sparkling displays and Christmas scenes. Glittering angels, trees, stars, and even a water skiing Santa Claus make every turn in the pathway a new delight. Leaving through the fantasyland tunnel of tiny white lights, visitors feel uplifted by a spirit of love and fun and can't help but smile when a little child tugs on his mother's hand and says, "I want to go again, Mommy, PLEASE, PLEASE, PLEASE!"

Just as dusk falls over the campus of TEXAS TECH UNIVERSITY in Lubbock the first Friday night in December, thousands of people gather in the Science Quadrangle and Memorial Circle awaiting the moment when the Saddle Tramps, Tech's spirit group, come streaming onto campus carrying red torches, signaling the start of the traditional "Carol of Lights." Christmas carols, led by Texas Tech's Musical Performance Department, fill the air as luminarias are lit around Memorial Circle. Then the Saddle Tramps douse the torches, and the magic moment arrives with simultaneous lighting of all the buildings, surrounding the awe-filled crowd with a wondrous glow of red, white, and yellow lights.

The CONCHO CHRISTMAS CELEBRATION, queen of West Texas Christmas lighting displays, transforms San Angelo's El Paseo de Santa Angela, the River Walk, and River Drive into a panoramic wonderland of sparkling Christmas scenes, such as an illuminated Santa Claus atop a stagecoach or towering toy soldiers standing guard near Celebration Bridge. Whether visitors walk or drive, each of the three trails leads to unforgettable Christmas splendor.

Our family especially loves the Christmas lights on the Hill Country Regional Tour because Llano's Lights and Spirit of Christmas are included on the tour. More than 10 miles of lights cover our 100-year-old County Courthouse area—it's pretty spectacular!

—**BETTY HIGGINS**, *Llano*

Our family loves Decatur's "Moonlight Madness" and the sleigh rides around the lighted Courthouse Square.

—**SUSAN WILLIAMS**, *Decatur*

The Paseo del Rio in San Antonio

We decorate the Blanco County Courthouse in Johnson City with over 100,000 lights. Ten volunteers decorate the courthouse, then we have others we jokingly refer to as "The Burning Bush Brigade" who decorate the trees in the surrounding area. Everything is so bright that people say they can read under the trees! We have a lighted parade, too, and everything in the parade has to have lights—even the llamas!

—MARY EARNEY, *Johnson City*

Every Christmas I decorate my almost life-sized cactus made out of old rusted barbed wire with over 200 miniature lights and put it in my yard with Mexican folk art figures.

—DOUG BEICH, *Grand Prairie*

Fantasy Park in Sealy looks like a fairyland lighted by beams of millions of tiny stars, with one giant star hovering above it all.

—PEGGY SPRADLEY,
Sealy Chamber of Commerce

Wearing an exquisite "gown" of glistening white cascading lights, BLANCO COUNTY COURTHOUSE becomes the crown jewel of JOHNSON CITY'S "LIGHTS SPECTACULAR—HILL COUNTRY–STYLE." As part of the annual Hill Country Regional Christmas Lighting tour, Johnson City puts on a magnificent, month-long display, lighting buildings throughout the downtown area—a beautiful Christmas present for Texas.

No Christmas season is complete in North Texas without a visit to Wichita Falls' spectacular "MSU-BURNS FANTASY OF LIGHTS." The campus of Midwestern State University comes alive in December with 29 brightly-lit scenes and over 18,000 lights outlining campus buildings, each year more breath-taking than the year before.

Nuestra Senora de la Concepcion del Socorro near El Paso

The Scurry County Courthouse on the square in Snyder has been decorated with Christmas lights almost every year since 1936 with the exception of the World War II years; 1949, when a major oil boom kept local people too busy to put up lights; and 1971, during renovations of the courthouse. A replica of a white buffalo, killed by J. Wright Mooar near Snyder in 1876, is on the corner of the square and gets a red wreath for Christmas each year.

—ALINE PARKS, *Snyder*

Our family loves the "Lights on Broadway" festival in Lubbock — music, LOTS of lights, and a night-time parade. We also enjoy Lubbock's Ranching Heritage Center's "Candlelight at the Ranch." Costumed volunteers "perform" in the houses demonstrating old-time ranch skills while spectators walk along luminaria-lit pathways.

—LEE WISE, Brownfield

One magical Christmas there was an ice storm that left the trees a fairyland. Our family always traveled from my maternal grandparent's home in North Louisiana to my father's mother's home in Texas. We traveled the backroads. About halfway there, we chanced to meet my aunt and her family who were headed for Mammaw's house. We honked, stopped, got out of our cars, and had a very chilly gift exchange as the sun shone down through the prisms of ice by the side of that country road.

—**Jane Clancy Debenport,**
Temple

A pine tree bears a snowy mantle
in Big Bend National Park

Holiday Events

WEST

Abilene
Abilene Convention
and Visitors Bureau
 (800) 727-7704

City Sidewalks, Parade and
Community Tree Lighting
 Beginning of December

Civic Center Community
Tree Lighting
 Beginning of December

KXTS-TV Christmas
Lights Parade
 Beginning of December

Drive Thru Celebration Park holiday scenes and animated displays
 December 1 – January 3

Alpine
Alpine Chamber of Commerce
 (915) 837-2326

Mountain Country Christmas
 2nd weekend in December

Andrews
Andrews Chamber of Commerce
 (915) 523-2695

Holly Jolly Weekend
 1st weekend in December

Christmas Chow Down
 1st Thursday in December

Lakeside Christmas Tree
Lighting and Caroling
 1st Friday in December

Arts and Crafts Show
 *1st Saturday and Sunday
 in December*

Lighted Christmas Parade
 1st Saturday in December

Christmas Time Festival of Homes
 1st Sunday in December

Anson
Anson Chamber of Commerce
 (915) 823-3259

Christmas Tour of Homes
 1st Saturday night in December

Christmas Tour of Businesses
 3rd Friday night in December

"Lights of Christmas" parade
 *2nd Saturday night
 in December*

Larry Chittenden
Cowboy Celebration
 *3rd Friday and Saturday
 in December*

The Cowboys' Christmas Ball
 *3rd Thursday, Friday and
 Saturday nights in December*

Ballinger
Ballinger Chamber of Commerce
 (915) 365-5611

Christmas in Olde Ballinger
 Saturday after Thanksgiving

Big Lake
Big Lake Chamber of Commerce
 (915) 884-2980

Christmas Downtown
 1st week in December

Big Spring
Big Spring Area
Chamber of Commerce
 (915) 263-7641

Big Spring Symphony Nutcracker
 Thanksgiving weekend

Festival of Lights
 1st weekend in December

Big Spring Herald Lighted
Christmas Parade
 1st Saturday in December

Living Christmas Tree at First
Church of the Nazarene
 1st weekend in December

Christmas Decorating Contest
 2nd week in December

Drive-Through Nativity
 2nd weekend in December

Tour of Homes
 2nd Sunday in December

Brownwood
Christmas Past and Present
 weekend before Thanksgiving

Colorado City
Colorado City Area
Chamber of Commerce
 (915) 728-3403

Christmas Parade
 1st weekend in December

Crowning of Little Miss and
Mister Merry Christmas
 1st weekend in December

Comanche
Comanche Chamber
of Commerce
 (915) 356-3233

Christmas Parade
 2nd Saturday in December

Christmas Tour of Homes
 2nd Saturday in December

"Old Cora Trade Day on the Square"
 2nd Saturday in December

Big Christmas Give-Away
 2nd Saturday in December

El Paso
Greater El Paso Convention
and Visitors Bureau
 (800) 351-6024

Christmas at Magoffin Home
 1st Sunday in December

Colors of Christmas
 1st Monday in December

Posada Navidena
 2nd Thursday in December

Holiday Pops
 2nd Saturday in December

Fort Davis
Fort Davis
Chamber of Commerce
 (915) 426-3015

Frontier Christmas
 1st weekend in December

Fort Davis
National Historic Site
Decorated for the holidays in
1880s style
 *mid-December – Monday after
 January 1*

Midland
Midland Convention
and Visitors Bureau
 (800) 624-6435

Christmas at the Mansion
 *Friday after Thanksgiving
 thru end of December*

Tree Lighting and Carol Sing
at Museum of the Southwest
 Friday after Thanksgiving

Midland College Holiday Evening
 1st Thursday in December

"World's Largest Christmas Party"
 1st Thursday in December

Jingle Bell Run
 1st Saturday in December

Merry, Merry Midland
Holiday Celebration
 1st Saturday in December

Holiday Pops, Midland-Odessa
Symphony Orchestra and Chorale
 1st Saturday in December

The Nutcracker Ballet
 2nd weekend in December

Odessa
Odessa Chamber of Commerce
 (915) 332-9111

Merry Market Place
 *2nd Thursday – Sunday
 in November*

Ye Olde Christmas Fair
 Thanksgiving weekend

Heritage Holiday Tree Lighting
 1st Thursday in December

Heritage Holiday Parade
 1st Saturday in December

White Pool House Open House
 *1st Saturday in December
 (after parade)*

"The Magic of Christmas" Midland-
Odessa Symphony and Choral
 1st Sunday in December

"Living Christmas Tree"
First Baptist Church
 2nd weekend in December

"First Night" Main Street Odessa
 New Year's Eve

Pecos
Community Christmas Parade
 1st Friday in December

Tour of Homes
 1st Friday in December

Christmas Parade
2nd Friday in December

Decorating of live trees at
West of the Pecos Museum
*1st weekend – 3rd week
in December*

Lighting of 500 Luminarias and
Chrismas party at the Museum
1st Saturday in December

San Angelo
San Angelo Convention
and Visitors Bureau
(800) 375-1206

Christmas at Fort Concho
1st weekend in December

Concho Christmas Celebration
month of December

Guild Craft Show
1st weekend in December

Snyder
Snyder Chamber of Commerce
(915) 573-3558

Lighted Christmas Parade
1st Saturday in December

Arts and Crafts Show
at Snyder Coliseum
1st weekend in December

Sweetwater
Sweetwater Chamber of Commerce
(915) 235-5488

Lighted "Night" Parade
Friday night after Thanksgiving

Trail of Lights
Thanksgiving to New Years

Christmas Arts and Crafts Show
1st weekend in December

Van Horn
Christmas Parade
1st Saturday in December

Wylie
Wylie Chamber of Commerce
(972) 442-2804

Annual Christmas Parade
1st Saturday in December

Tour of Homes/Carriage Rides
1st Saturday in December

Tree Lighting
1st Saturday in December

CENTRAL

Austin
Austin Convention
and Visitors Bureau
(800) 888-8287

A Christmas Affair
3rd week in November

Chuy's "Children Giving
to Children" Parade
Saturday after Thanksgiving

Victorian Christmas on 6th Street
Thanksgiving weekend

The Colors of Christmas
at Bass Concert Hall
last Sunday in November

Sami Arts and Crafts Affaire
1st weekend in December

Christmas Market–
German-Heritage Society
1st weekend in December

Jingle 5K Run
1st Saturday in December

Lone Star of David: A Celebration
of Texas Jewish Music
1st Saturday in December

Carols on the Terrace–Umlauf
Sculpture Garden and Museum
1st Sunday in December

Christmas at the French Legation
1st Sunday in December

Texas Christmas Traditions
1st Sunday in December

Zilker tree lighting ceremony
1st Sunday in December

Christmas Candlelight Tours
2nd weekend in December

Armadillo Christmas Bazaar
*2nd and 3rd weekends in
December*

Yulefest—Annual Trail of Lights
in Zilker Park
*2nd weekend in December
to December 24*

Trail of Lights 5K in Zilker Park
2nd Saturday in December

O. Henry Victorian Christmas
2nd Sunday in December

Christmas Celebration in main
rotunda of Texas State Capitol
Saturday before Christmas

Sing-It Yourself Messiah at
St. Matthew's Episcopal Church
Sunday before Christmas

New Year's Celebration
on Sixth Street
New Year's Eve

Candlelight Tours Jourdan
Bachman Pioneer Farm
mid-December

Bastrop
Bastop Chamber of Commerce
(512) 321-2419

Thanksgiving Arts and Crafts Show
*Friday and Saturday of
Thanksgiving weekend*

Christmas parade
1st Thursday in December

Holiday Homes Tour
2nd Saturday in December

New Year's Gala
December 31st

Bellville
Bellville Chamber of Commerce
(409) 865-3407

"Small Town Christmas"
1st weekend in December

"Snow Night"
1st Friday in December

American Cancer Society Home Tour
1st weekend in December

Belton
Belton Area Chamber of Commerce
(254) 939-3551

Nature in Lights
*2nd week in November
thru January 3*

Arts and Crafts Christmas Market
1st weekend in December

Parade of Lights
1st Sunday in December

Blanco
Blanco Chamber of Commerce
(210) 833-5101

Lighting of Courthouse and Square
Thanksgiving weekend

Lights of the Season
Thanksgiving thru December

Taste of the Season
1st Friday in December

Tour of Homes Dinner and Tour
2nd Thursday in December

Merry Merchants Market
2nd weekend in December

LBJ Heartland Council
Holiday Market
2nd weekend in December

Boerne
Greater Boerne Area
Chamber of Commerce
(830) 249-8000 or
(888) 842-8080

Weihnachtsfest Parade
1st Friday in December

Breakfast with Santa
1st Saturday in December

Oma's Christmas Craft Fair
1st weekend in December

Follow the Star Christmas Drive-Thru
Thanksgiving to January 1

Brenham
Brenham/Washington County
Chamber of Commerce
(409) 836-3695

Poinsettia Celebration
weekend before Thanksgiving

Downtown Christmas Stroll
1st weekend in December

Cowboy Christmas Gathering
1st weekend in December

Brookshire
Brookshire-Pattison
Chamber of Commerce
(281) 375-8100

Christmas Festival
1st weekend in December

Bryan/College Station
Bryan/College Station
Chamber of Commerce
(800) 777-8292

Holiday on the Brazos
1st 3 weeks in December

Burnet
Burnet Chamber of Commerce
(512) 756-4297

Christmas on the Square
1st Saturday in December

Main Street Bethlehem
1st and 2nd weekends in December

Christmas at Ft. Croghan
*1st Saturday thru 2nd Saturday
in December*

Calvert
Calvert Chamber of Commerce
(409) 364-2559

Victorian Homes Tour
1st weekend in December

Chappell Hill
Country Christmas
2nd Saturday in December

Cleveland
Greater Cleveland
Chamber of Commerce
(281) 592-8786

Annual Christmas Parade
1st Saturday in December

Columbus
Columbus Convention
and Visitors Bureau
(409) 732-5135

Christmas on the Colorado
1st weekend in December

Mary Elizabeth Hopkins
Santa Claus Museum
*open Thursday – Saturday
year-round*

Eden
Eden Chamber of Commerce
(915) 869-3336

"Moonlight Sale"—Sales, Santa
Claus, lights, music, and chili supper
1st Thursday in December

Elgin
Lights of the Blacklands
month of December

Flatonia
Flatonia Chamber of Commerce
(361) 865-3920

Christmas Homes Tour
2nd weekend in December

White Christmas in Flatonia
2nd weekend in December

Blue Santa Golf Tournament
December

Fredericksburg
Fredericksburg
Chamber of Commerce
(830) 997-6523

Regional Christmas Lighting Tour
*Friday after Christmas thru
month of December*

Weihnachten in Fredericksburg
*10 days beginning 1st Friday
in December*

Santa Claus Parade
1st Saturday in December

Kinderfest
1st Saturday in December

Christmas Candlelight Tour of Homes
2nd Saturday in December

Our Lady of Guadalupe Festival
2nd Saturday in December

Zweite Weihnachten
day after Christmas

Boxing Day Celebration
day after Christmas

Georgetown
Georgetown Convention
and Visitors Bureau
(800) 436-8696

Historic Downtown Courthouse
Holiday Lights Display
December annually

Christmas Stroll, Downtown Square
1st Saturday in December

Multi-Media Art Show
and Christmas Market
1st weekend in December

Holiday Home Tour
2nd weekend in December

Market Days, Downtown Square
2nd Saturday in December

**Hill Country Christmas
Lighting Tour**
Eleven towns dazzle visitors
*Thanksgiving weekend
thru New Year's*
Blanco, Bulverde, Burnet,
Dripping Springs, Fredericksburg,
Goldthwaite, Johnson City,
Llano, Marble Falls, Mason,
Round Mountain

Hillsboro
Hillsboro Chamber of Commerce
(254) 582-2481

Holiday Hillsboro
throughout December

Hutto
Hutto Chamber of Commerce
(512) 846-7077

Nativity Scene
United Methodist Church
month of December

Lucia Celebration
Hutto Lutheran Church
2nd Sunday in December

Santa Comes to Hutto
1st Sunday in December

Lights of the Blackland Tours
month of December

Johnson City
Johnson City Chamber of Commerce
(210) 868-7684

Lights Spectacular, Hill Country Style
*Thanksgiving weekend
thru January 1*

Kerrville
Kerrville Area Chamber of Commerce
(830) 896-1155

Christmas on the Square
1st Saturday in December

Twilight Country Christmas Tour
2nd Saturday in December

Hill Country Youth Orchestra
Christmas Concert
2nd Monday in December

Community Messiah Sing
3rd Sunday in December

Killeen
Killeen Convention
and Visitors Bureau
(254) 526-9551

Nature in Lights at Fort Hood
mid-November thru December

Holiday Lighting Celebration
2nd weekend in December

Kingsland
Merchants Christmas Open House
1st two weeks in December

Christmas Tree Lighting
2nd Saturday in December

La Grange
La Grange Area
Chamber of Commerce
(409) 968-5756

Santa's Lane of Lights
*Fridays and Saturdays ending
last weekend in December*

Candlelight singing and
lighting of courthouse
1st Friday in December

Country Christmas in Fayetteville
1st Saturday in December

Lampasas
Lampasas County
Chamber of Commerce
(512) 556-5172

Community Christmas
December 1 – January 1

Carol of Lights
1st Friday in December

Llano
"Lights Aglow"
Thanksgiving weekend

Santa's Big Night
Saturday after Thanksgiving

"Parade of Lights"
1st Saturday in December

Lockhart
Holiday Homes Tour
1st Saturday in December

Luckenbach
Luckenbach Turkey Trot,
Walk, Run, Bike, and Dance
Saturday after Thanksgiving

Cowboy Christmas Ball
day after Christmas

Madisonville
Christmas "Night" Parade of Lights
1st weekend in December

Marble Falls/Lake LBJ
Marble Falls–Lake LBJ
Chamber of Commerce
(830) 693-4449 or
(800) 759-8178

Walkway of Lights
*Friday before Thanksgiving
thru January 1*

Marlin
Marlin Chamber of Commerce
(254) 883-2171

Chamber Lighted Parade
1st Thursday in December

Miracle on Main Street
1st Saturday in December

Mason
Mason County
Chamber of Commerce
(915) 347-5758

Light Up Our Town
Saturday after Thanksgiving

Tannenbaum Time Craft Show
Saturday after Thanksgiving

Christmas Luminary
1st Sunday in December

Chamber of Commerce Homes Tour
2nd Saturday in December

Navasota
Christmas in Navasota
1st weekend in December

New Braunfels
The Greater New Braunfels
Chamber of Commerce
(830) 625-2385

The Holiday River of Lights
mid-November to early January

Weihnachtsmarket
3rd weekend in November

Wassailfest
1st Thursday in December

Glowfest Holiday Hot Air
Balloon Festival
weekend before Thanksgiving

Visit with St. Nicholas
1st Saturday in December

Candlelight Tour
1st Saturday in December

Old Gruene Christmas
Market Days Festival
1st weekend in December

Arts and Crafts, Town Lighting,
and Cowboy Kringle Christmas
Tour of Homes
2nd Saturday in December

Red McCombs Jingle Bell 5K Run
2nd Saturday in December

A Christmas Journey—German historic Christmas experiences in Texas
2nd Sunday in December

Caroling on the Plaza
3rd Thursday in December

Harvest from the Heart
3rd Monday in December

Pflugerville
Greater Pflugerville
Chamber of Commerce
(512) 251-7799

Holidays at Heritage Park
1st weekend in November

Christmas on Main Street
1st Monday in December

Salado
Salado Chamber of Commerce
(254) 947-5040

Christmas Stroll
1st and 2nd weekends in December

Salado Historical Society
Holiday Homes Tour
1st weekend in December

"A Christmas Carol"
1st and 2nd weekends
in December

San Marcos
San Marcos Area
Chamber of Commerce
(512) 393-5900

Sights and Sounds of Christmas
1st Thursday, Friday, and
Saturday in December

Historic Holiday Homes Tour
1st weekend in December

Sealy
Sealy Chamber of Commerce
(409) 885-3222

Arts and Crafts Show
1st Saturday in December

Christmas Home Tour
1st Saturday in December

A Taste of Christmas
1st Saturday in December

Lights On at Fantasy Park
1st Saturday in December

Fantasy of Lights Parade
1st Saturday in December

Mistletoe and Magic
dinner and dance
1st Saturday night in December

Stonewall
Stonewall Chamber of Commerce
(830) 644-2735

Stonewall Heritage Society
Christmas Gala
1st Saturday in December

LBJ State and National Historical
Christmas Tree Lighting
Sunday evening before Christmas

Taylor
Taylor Chamber of Commerce
(512) 352-6364

Christmas Lights at Heritage Square
Thanksgiving week through
January 1

Christmas Parade of Lights
1st Thursday in December

Lights of the Blackland
Thanksgiving thru New Year's Day

Temple
Temple Chamber of Commerce
(254) 773-2105

Oldest Lighted Christmas Parade
1st Monday in December

Thorndale
Thorndale Area
Chamber of Commerce
(254) 697-4979

Christmas Lighting
Sunday following Thanksgiving

Santa Claus Christmas Parade
1st Saturday in December

Santa House Pictures
after parade

Blackland Tour of Lights
Sunday after Thanksgiving
thru December

Waco
Greater Waco
Chamber of Commerce
(254) 752-6551

Evergreen Acres Christmas
Tree Farm Celebration
Thanksgiving weekend

Christmas Tree Lighting
1st Thursday in December

Christmas on the Brazos
1st weekend in December

Cowboy Christmas Ball
Saturday night before Christmas

SOUTH

Alamo-La Bahia Corridor
"Christmas Along the Corridor"
1st Sat. in December
Pony Express Courier Run,
including towns of Goliad,
Hobson, Falls City, Poth,
Floresville, Pleasanton, Runge,
Helena, Panna Maria, Stockdale,
Seguin, Sutherland Springs,
Adkins, La Vernia, Elmendorf,
and San Antonio

Angleton
Angleton Chamber of Commerce
(409) 849-6443

Christmas on the Square
1st Friday evening in December

Bay City
Bay City Chamber of
Commerce and Agriculture
(409) 245-8333

Parade of Lights
1st Tuesday in December

Tour of Homes by
Matagorda County Museum
1st Sunday in December

Christmas Market Days on the Square
1st Sunday in December

Beeville
Bee County Chamber of Commerce
(512) 358-3267

Beeville Market Day/Christmas Show
1st Saturday in December

Christmas Tour of Homes
2nd Sunday

Bishop
Bishop Chamber of Commerce
(361) 584-2214

"Christmas in the Park"
1st Friday in December

Brazosport
Brazosport Area
Chamber of Commerce
(409) 265-2505

Festival of Lights
Saturday before Thanksgiving

Holiday on the Brazos
1st Friday in December

Christmas Tidings on the Gulf,
Quintana Park
month of December

Light Up Christmas Festival
1st Saturday in December

Christmas in the Park
2nd week in December

Christmas Boat Parade
2nd Saturday in December

Christmas Bird Count
in Brazosport
Between Christmas
and New Year's

Brownsville
Brownsville Convention
and Visitors Bureau
(800) 626-2639

Tree Lighting at Convention
and Visitors Bureau
end of November

Chamber of Commerce
Christmas Parade
1st week in December

Castroville
Castroville Chamber of Commerce
(830) 538-3142 or
(800) 778-6775

Old-Fashioned Christmas
1st Saturday in December

Corpus Christi
Greater Corpus Christi
Business Alliance
(361) 881-1888

Annual Central Power and
Light Harbor Lights Festival
1st weekend in December

Holiday Forest
1st weekend in December

Del Rio
Del Rio Chamber of Commerce
(830) 775-3551

Official City Christmas Tree
Lighting and Christmas Night Parade
1st week in December

Parade of Trees
1st two weekends in December

Edinburg
Edinburg Chamber of Commerce
(210) 383-4974

Celebration of Lights
1st week in December

Best Home Decorating Contest
1st – 3rd week in December

Tamalada—Tamales at the Depot
1st week in December

El Campo
"Carol of Lights" Christmas
Parade and Tree Lighting
1st Thursday in December

Home Lighting Contest
2nd week in December

Goliad
Goliad Chamber of Commerce
Historical Commission
(800) 848-8674

Christmas in Goliad
1st Friday and Saturday
in December

Las Posadas
1st weekend in December

Gonzales
Gonzales Chamber of Commerce
(830) 672-6532

Christmas Candlelight Tour
of Historic Homes
1st weekend in December

Christmas in the Cradle
of Texas Independence
November and December

Hallettsville
Hallettsville Chamber of
Commerce and Agriculture
(361) 798-2662

Festival of Lights
Saturday and Sunday following
Thanksgiving

Holiday Tour of Homes
1st Saturday in December

Lions Club Arts and Crafts Show
1st Sunday in December

Hondo
Hondo Area Chamber of Commerce
(830) 426-3037

Christmas in God's Country
Saturday before Thanksgiving

Arts and Crafts, Kiddie Parade,
Entertainment, Lighting of
Downtown, Parade, Christmas
Cards on the Highway (Hwy. 90)
Saturday before Thanksgiving
thru Christmas

Kingsville
Kingsville Convention
and Visitors Bureau
(361) 592-8516 or
(800) 333-5032

King Ranch, Ranch Hand Breakfast
3rd Saturday in November

La Posada—Parade of Lights
and Pastoral Parade
1st Saturday in December

Angel 5K Run/Walk
1st Saturday in December

Christmas Tour of Homes
1st Sunday in December

Lessons and Carols
1st Sunday in December

Christmas Tree Forest
*end of November thru
mid-December*

Lighting Ceremony
end of November

Laredo
Laredo Convention
and Visitors Bureau
(956) 795-2200 or
(800) 361-3360

Christmas Tree Lighting Ceremony
1st Saturday in December

Jaycees Christmas Parade
1st Sunday in December

McAllen
McAllen Convention
and Visitors Bureau
(956) 682-2871 or
(800) 250-2591

McAllen's Candlelight Posada
*1st Friday and Saturday
in December*

Moulton
Moulton Chamber of Commerce
(512) 596-7205

Chamber of Commerce
Christmas Program
Last Sunday in November

Palacios
Lighting of the Palm, Holiday
on the Main, and Santa's Arrival
weekend before Thanksgiving

Christmas Lighting Contest
2nd/3rd week in December

Pearland
Pearland/Hobby Area
Chamber of Commerce
(281) 485-3634

Night Time Christmas Parade
1st Saturday in December

Walk on Broadway
Monday following parade

Port Isabel
Port Isabel
Chamber of Commerce
(956) 943-2262 or
(800) 527-6102

Laguna Madre Lighted
Christmas Boat Parade
1st Saturday in December

Port Lavaca
Port Lavaca-Calhoun County
Chamber of Commerce
(512) 552-2959

Festival of Lights Christmas Parade
1st weekend in December

Port Neches
Port Neches Chamber of Commerce
(409) 722-9154

Christmas on the Neches—boat
parade, carnival, fireworks and more
1st weekend of December

Richmond
Fort Bend Museum Association
Moore Home Candlelight Tour
1st weekend in December

"Campfire Christmas" at
Historic George Ranch
*2nd and 3rd weekends
in December*

Rockport-Fulton
Rockport-Fulton Area
Chamber of Commerce
(512) 729-6445

Coastal Celebration of Lights
1st Saturday in December

Lighting of the Children's Tree
1st Saturday in December

Holly Days Festival in
Downtown Rockport
1st Saturday in December

Lighted Boat Parade
1st Saturday in December

Christmas at the Mansion
early in December

Rosenburg
Rosenburg Revitalization
Association
(281) 342-4664

Christmas Magic
Saturday after Thanksgiving

San Antonio
San Antonio Convention
and Visitors Bureau
(210) 270-6700 or
(800) 447-3372

Fiesta de las Luminarias
*on Riverwalk 1st 3 weekends
in December*

Rivercenter Christmas Pageant
1st 3 weekends in December

Holiday in the Park
month of December

Botanical Gardens Christmas
Tree Contest
1st Saturday in December

Kristkindlmarket
1st Saturday in December

King William Holiday Home Tour
1st Saturday in December

Arrival of Pony Express Riders
at Fort Sam Houston
1st Saturday in December

La Pastorela
*2nd Friday and Saturday
in December*

Las Posadas on Riverwalk
2nd Sunday in December

Gran Posada de San Antonio
week before Christmas

Los Pastores
*1st Saturday after Christmas
(except December 26 or 31 or
January 1 — held then 1st
Saturday after January 1)*

San Benito
San Benito Chamber of Commerce
(956) 399-5321

Longest Lighted Christmas Parade
1st Saturday in December

Santa arriving via helicopter
1st Saturday in December

San Ygnacio
Historical Christmas Tours
1st Sunday in December

Seguin
Seguin Area Chamber of Commerce
(830) 379-6382

"A Holiday Stroll in Central Park"
*1st Thursday, Friday, and
Saturday in December*

A Taste of Christmas Past at
Sebastopol Historical Park
1st Saturday in December

Living Windows
1st weekend in December

Pony Express Arrival
1st Saturday in December

Yulefest Arts and Crafts
1st Sunday in December

Historic Homes Tour
1st Sunday in December

Christmas Vespers at
Texas Lutheran University
1st weekend in December

South Padre Island
South Padre Island
Convention and Visitors Bureau
(956) 761-6433 or
(800) 767-2373

Lighting of the Island
and Christmas Tree
Thanksgiving weekend

Santa's Treasure Chest
of Arts and Crafts
Thanksgiving weekend

Annual Island of Lights Street Parade
1st Friday in December

Sweeny
Sweeny Chamber of Commerce
(409) 548-3249

A Victorian Christmas
1st weekend in December

Taft
Taft Chamber of Commerce
(512) 528-3230

Christmas Parade
1st Saturday in December

Uvalde
Uvalde Chamber of
Commerce and Visitors Bureau
(830) 278-3361

City of Lights
Fri. after Thanksgiving

Holiday Arts and Crafts
Saturday after Thanksgiving

Victoria
Greater Victoria Area
Chamber of Commerce
(361) 573-5277

Lighted Christmas Parade
1st Saturday in December

West Columbia
West Columbia
Chamber of Commerce
(409) 345-3921

Christmas at Varner Hogg
Plantation State Park
1st Saturday in December

A Cowboy Christmas
1st Saturday in December

West Columbia's
"Winter Wonderland"
1st weekend in December

NORTH CENTRAL

Arlington
Arlington Convention
and Visitors Bureau
(800) 342-4305

Young Country Christmas
Fireworks to Music
*Saturday of Thanksgiving
weekend*

Johnnie High's Country
Christmas Show
1st 3 weeks in December

Feast of Carols
1st week in December

Asian Culture Holiday Cabaret
1st Friday in December

Celebration of Lights
1st weekend in December

Six Flags Over Texas
Holiday in the Park
month of December

Community sing-along and fireworks
Sunday before Christmas

Tarrant County Toy Run
Sunday before Christmas

Bedford
International Tree Celebration
Thanksgiving week thru January 1

Bonham
Bonham Area Chamber of Commerce
(903) 583-4811

Tour Wishing Star
Christmas Tree Farm
weekend after Thanksgiving

A Taste of Christmas
1st 3 weekends in December

Carrollton
Carrollton Chamber of Commerce
(972) 416-6600

Lights of Christmas
December 1

"Old-Fashioned Christmas"
1st Friday in December

Christmas Parade and Lighting
1st Saturday in December

Celina
Greater Celina
Chamber of Commerce
(972) 382-3736

"Holidays in Celina"
Thursday before Thanksgiving

Cleburne
Cleburne Chamber of Commerce
(817) 645-2455

"Whistlestop Christmas"
*1st Friday and Saturday and
2nd Saturday in December*

St. Nicholas Fest
1st weekend in December

Candlelight Tour of Homes
1st Saturday in December

Corsicana
Corsicana Area
Chamber of Commerce
(903) 874-4731

Festival of Lights
1st Saturday in December

Dallas
Dallas Convention
and Visitors Bureau
(800) 232-5527 or
(214) 571-1301

Holiday Tree Lighting Festival—
West End Marketplace
Friday after Thanksgiving

Christmas at the Arboretum
and DeGolyer Mansion
late November thru Christmas

Galleria Holiday Kickoff with
"Mistle Toes," the ice-skating Santa
late November

Fair Park Holiday Lights
Month of December

Neiman Marcus/Adolphus
Children's Parade
1st week of December

Candlelight Tour Old City Park
Early to mid-December

Christmas at the Superpops
mid-December

White Rock Marathon
mid-December

Jingle Bell Run 5K,
Downtown Dallas
mid-December

Decatur
Decatur Chamber of Commerce
(940) 627-3107

Lucky Seven
Day after Thanksgiving

"Moonlight Madness" lights,
parade, sleigh rides, and shopping
1st Saturday in December

Tour of Homes
1st Saturday in December

Denison
Denison Area
Chamber of Commerce
(903) 465-1551

Christmas Parade
1st Thursday in December

Holiday Tour of Homes
1st Saturday in December

Old-Fashioned Christmas
at Frontier Village
1st Sunday in December

Denton
Denton Convention
and Visitors Bureau
(940) 382-7895 or
(888) 381-1818

Christmas Tree Forest
month of December

UNT One O'Clock Lab Band
Annual Fall Concert
3rd week in November

Holiday Lighting of
Downtown Denton
1st Thursday in December

AAUW Annual
Christmas Home Tour
1st Sunday in December

Ennis
Ennis Convention
and Visitors Bureau
(972) 878-4748

Kolache Christmas and
Czech Culture Celebration
1st Saturday in December

Night Holiday Parade
1st Saturday in December

Downtown Christmas Celebration
1st Saturday in December

Holiday Tour of Homes
and Celebration
1st Sunday in December

Forney
Forney Area Chamber of Commerce
(972) 564-2233

Christmas in the Park
1st Saturday in December

Christmas tree lighting in Bell Park
1st Thursday in December

Forney Tour of Historic Homes
*2nd weekend in December
(every other year)*

Fort Worth
Fort Worth Convention
and Visitors Bureau
(817) 336-8791 or
(800) 433-5747

Parade of Lights
Friday after Thanksgiving

Stockyards Christmas Parade
Saturday after Thanksgiving

Christmas in the Stockyards
December annually

Christmas in Sundance Square
December annually

The T Tour of Lights
December annually

Zoobilee of Lights at
the Fort Worth Zoo
December annually (except 1999)

Frisco
Have a Merry Main Street
1st Friday in December

Garland
Garland Convention
and Visitors Bureau
(972) 205-2749

Christmas Tree Lighting
Christmas on the Square
1st Monday in December

Gatesville
Gatesville Area Chamber of
Commerce and Agribusiness
(254) 865-2617

Christmas Parade
1st Saturday in December

Granbury
Granbury Convention
and Visitors Bureau
(817) 573-5548 or
(800) 950-2212

Country Christmas Celebration
and Lighted Christmas Parade
day after Thanksgiving

Lone Star Lights
*Thanksgiving weekend
through December*

Enchanted Forest
*Saturday after Thanksgiving
and first weekend in December*

Candlelight Tour of Homes
1st weekend in December

Grand Prairie
City of Grand Prairie
(972) 237-8140

"Winter Wonderland"
City Hall Plaza
*1st Saturday in December –
January 4*

"Light Up Grand Prairie"
decorating contest/display
month of December

Grapevine
Grapevine Convention
and Visitors Bureau
(800) 457-6338

Carol of Lights
Monday before Parade of Lights

Parade of Lights
1st Thursday in December

Whistlestop Christmas
1st 2 weekends in December

Harlingen
Harlingen Area
Chamber of Commerce
(956) 423-5440 or
(800) 531-7346

Christmas Tree Lighting
1st week in December

Arroyo Colorado
Christmas Lighting
1st Thursday in December

Jaycees and Downtown
Improvement District
Christmas Parade
1st Friday in December

Piñata Festival at Gutierrez Park
after parade

Irving
Irving Convention
and Visitors Bureau
(972) 252-7476 or
(800) 2-Irving

Santa's Cruise on the
Mandalay Canal
December

Annual Christmas Classic Run
1st week in December

Traditional Holiday Concert
mid-December

Kaufman
Greater Kaufman
Chamber of Commerce
(972) 932-3118

Christmas on the Square
1st Thursday in December

Lancaster
Lancaster Chamber of Commerce
(972) 227-2579

Heritage Park Tree Lighting
1st week in December

Christmas Parade
1st Saturday in December

Second Saturday on the Square
2nd Saturday in December

Volleyball Christmas Classic
2nd Saturday in December

Breakfast with Santa
Saturday before Christmas

Kids Christmas Camp
*2 weeks during Christmas
school vacation*

Lewisville
Lewisville Old Town
Business Association
(972) 436-3556

Old Town Christmas Stroll
1st weekend in December

Mansfield
Mansfield Chamber of Commerce
(817) 473-7654

Christmas in the Park
1st Friday in December

McKinney
McKinney Convention
and Visitors Bureau
(888) 649-8499

Dickens of a Christmas on the
historic downtown square
*Friday and Saturday after
Thanksgiving*

Old-Fashioned
Christmas Home Tour
1st weekend in December

Mineral Wells
Mineral Wells Area
Chamber of Commerce
(940)325-2557 or
(800)252-MWTX

Crazy Water Christmas:
The Spirit of Christmas Past
1st Wednesday in December

Crystal Christmas
month of December

Christmas Parade
beginning of December

Zonta Holiday Home Tour
1st Sunday in December

Lighting of Baker Hotel and Tree
Saturday after Thanksgiving

Nocona
Nocona Chamber of Commerce
(940) 825-3526

Nocona Downtown Christmas
1st weekend of December

Palestine
Palestine Convention
and Visitors Bureau
(800) 659-3484

Dogwood Historic Homes Tour
1st weekend in December

Christmas Parade
1st Saturday in December

Victorian Christmas (train ride)
month of December

Richardson
Richardson Convention
and Visitors Bureau
(972) 234-4141 or
(800) 777-8001

Women's Club of Richardson
Holiday Home Tour
2nd weekend in November

Christmas Parade
1st Saturday in December

Richardson Tree Lighting
Ceremony at Civic Center
1st Saturday in December

"Santa's Village"
*1st weekend thru 3rd
weekend in December*

Sherman
Sherman Chamber of Commerce
(903) 893-1184

Annual Sherman Jaycees
Christmas Parade
December 1

Christmas Pilgrimage
2nd Sunday in December

Waxahachie
Waxahachie Chamber
of Commerce
(972) 937-2390

Candlelight Home Tour
3 weekends after Thanksgiving

Bethlehem Revisited
1st two weekends in December

Wichita Falls
Wichita Falls Board of
Commerce and Industry
(940) 723-2741

Christmas Magic
1st weekend in November

Christmas Bazaar and Antique Sale
2nd weekend in November

Midwestern State University
Fantasy of Lights
*1st weekend in December
to December 31*

Wichita Falls Ballet—Nutcracker
1st weekend in December

Christmas at Kell House
month of December

PANHANDLE

Amarillo
Amarillo Convention
and Visitors Council
(800) 692-1338

Christmas Parade
1st Saturday in December

Night of Lights
Month of December

Canyon
Canyon Chamber of Commerce
(806) 655-7815

"Canyon Christmas Open House"
2nd weekend in November

Christmas Luncheon
and Style Show
3rd Friday in November

Panhandle-Plains
Historical Museum's
"Old-Fashioned Christmas"
1st weekend in December

Victorian Christmas
1st weekend in December

Dalhart
Dalhart Area
Chamber of Commerce
(806) 249-5646

Christmas in the Park
Living Christmas Tree
1st Saturday in December

Dumas
Dumas/Moore County
Chamber of Commerce
(806) 935-2123

Kandy Kane Lane on Main
throughout December

Christmas Sidewalk Festival
Friday after Thanksgiving

Light Up Dumas
Friday after Thanksgiving

Crabb Art Center
Holiday Open House
1st weekend in December

Moore Co. Historical Museum
Open House
1st week in December

Christmas Light Contest
3rd week in December

Graham
Graham Chamber of Commerce
(940) 549-3355

Starlight Extravaganza
*1st Thursday, Friday, and
Saturday in December*

Christmas Parade
1st Saturday in December

CLSC Tour of Homes
2nd Wednesday in December

The Living Christmas Tree
2nd week in December

Hamlin
Hamlin Chamber of Commerce
(915) 576-3501

Big Green Christmas
1st Thursday evening in December

Lubbock
Lubbock Convention
and Tourism Bureau
(806) 747-5232 or
(800) 692-4035

"Lights on Broadway"
1st Friday in December

"Carol of Lights" at Texas Tech
1st Friday in December

An Orchard Christmas
1st Saturday in December

Ranching Heritage Center's
"Candlelight at the Ranch"
2nd weekend in December

Memphis
Memphis Chamber of Commerce
(806) 259-3144

Christmas Tour of Homes
2nd Sunday in December

Christmas Tree Forest
*2nd weekend in December
thru following Saturday*

Pampa
Greater Pampa Area
Chamber of Commerce
(806) 669-3241

Celebration of Lights
*3rd Friday of November
thru December 31*

Chamber of Commerce
Christmas Parade
1st Saturday in December

"The Nutcracker Ballet"
1st Saturday in December

Holiday Home Tour
1st Sunday in December

Shephard's Helping Hands
"Festival of Trees"
1st Saturday in December

Plainview
Plainview Chamber of Commerce
(806) 296-7431

Christmas Parade and
Symphony Concert
1st Thursday in December

"American Family Christmas" musical presentation by Wayland Baptist University
2nd Thursday in December

Slaton
Slaton Chamber of Commerce
(806) 828-6238

Christmas Parade and Promotion
1st Saturday in December

Women's Division of the
Chamber of Commerce
Annual Tour of Homes
1st Sunday in December

EAST

Beaumont
Beaumont Convention
and Visitors Bureau
(800) 392-4401

Children's Holiday Party at
the Downtown Museums
1st Thursday in December

Tour of Homes
1st Saturday in December

Candlelight Tour
1st Sunday in December

Christmas at Gladys City
2nd Sunday in December

Oaks Old Town
Historic Homes Tour
2nd Sunday in December

Christmas Memories
and Traditions at
McFaddin-Ward House
1st Thursday in December

Christmas at McFaddin-Ward
1st 3 Sundays in December

Canton
Canton Chamber of Commerce
(903) 567-2991

Christmas Parade
2nd Saturday in December

Clear Lake
Christmas Boat Parade
on Clear Lake
2nd Saturday in December

Coldspring
Coldspring Chamber
of Commerce
(409) 653-2184

Town Lighting
Saturday after Thanksgiving

Christmas on the Square
2nd Saturday in December

Commerce
Commerce Chamber
of Commerce
(903) 886-3950

Celebration of Lights
and Christmas Parade
1st Thursday in December

Conroe
Greater Conroe
Chamber of Commerce
(800) 283-6645

Toyland on the Square
Christmas Parade
1st Friday in December

Annual Christmas Parade
1st Saturday in December

Christmas in Old Montgomery
2nd Saturday in December

Live Nativity and
Bethlehem Market
2nd weekend in December

Christmas Carol Cruise
on the Southern Empress
week before Christmas

Edgewood
Edgewood Historical Society
(903) 896-1940

Log Cabin Christmas
Bazaar and Festival
2nd Saturday in November

Galena Park
Galena Park
Chamber of Commerce
(713) 672-6443

"Let's Light Up Galena Park"
*2nd Saturday in December
at dusk*

Galveston
Galveston Convention
and Vistors Bureau
(409) 763-4311 or
(800) 351-4236

Galveston Harbor
Parade of Lights
*Saturday of Thanksgiving
weekend*

Dickens on the Strand
1st weekend in December

Christmas by Candlelight at
Samuel May Williams Home
*evenings 1st weekend
in December*

Dickens Feast at Ashton Villa
1st weekend in December

Morning Tea at Ashton Villa
1st weekend in December

West India Dock
1st weekend in December

Holly and Candlelight
2nd weekend in December

Gilmer
Upshur County
Chamber of Commerce
(903) 843-2413

Yulefest
1st Saturday of December

Houston
Greater Houston Convention
and Visitors Bureau
(713) 227-3100 or
(800) 4HOUSTON

Nutcracker Market
at the Astro Arena
mid-November

Uptown Tree Lighting Ceremony
Thanksgiving night

Miracle on Main Street
*Thanksgiving weekend
thru December*

Candlelight Tour at
Sam Houston Park
2nd week in December

Bayou Bend Candlelight
Open House
2nd and 3rd Friday in December

Huntsville/Walker County
Huntsville-Walker County
Chamber of Commerce
(409) 295-8113 or
(800) 289-0389

"Trail of Lights"
November and December

Christmas Parade
1st Saturday in December

Christmas Candlelight Tour at the
Sam Houston Memorial Museum
2nd Saturday in December

Jefferson
Christmas Candlelight Tour
*1st and 2nd weekends
in December*

Kilgore
Kilgore Chamber of Commerce
(903) 984-5022

Annual Chamber of
Commerce Christmas Parade
Tuesday following Thanksgiving

Kirbyville
Kirbyville Area Heritage Society
(409) 423-4634

Christmas in the Park
Saturday after Thanksgiving

Longview
Longview Convention
and Visitors Bureau
(903) 753-3281

Living History Christmas
1st Saturday in December

Lighted Christmas Parade
1st Friday in December

Light Up Longview-Downtown
month of December

Lufkin
Lufkin Convention
and Visitors Bureau
(409) 634-6644

Holiday on the Square
1st Saturday after Thanksgiving

An Evening in Old Bethlehem
2nd weekend in December

Marshall
Greater Marshall
Chamber of Commerce
(903) 935-7868

Wonderland of Lights
*day before Thanksgiving–
end of December*

Wonderland of Lights
Historic Homes Tour
*Thanksgiving thru 3rd
weekend in December*

Lighted Christmas Parade
1st Saturday in December

Cowboy Christmas Celebration
2nd Saturday in December

Victorian Candlelight Tour
1st 3 Saturdays in December

Montgomery
Christmas in Old Montgomery
2nd Saturday in December

Nacogdoches
Nacogdoches Convention
and Visitors Bureau
(409) 564-7351

Nine Flags Christmas Festival
"Oldest Christmas in Texas"
1st weekend in December

Candlelight Tour of Homes
2nd Saturday in December

Jingle Bell Run
3rd Saturday in December

Nederland
Nederland Chamber
of Commerce
(409) 722-0279

Christmas Parade
1st Tuesday in December

Newton
Newton County
Chamber of Commerce
(409) 379-5527

125

Festival of Lights
*Saturday after Thanksgiving
thru January 2*

Paris
Paris Chamber of Commerce
and Visitors Center
(903) 784-2501 or
(800) PARIS TX

Christmas at the Maxey House
1st Sunday in December

Paris Council of Garden Clubs
Christmas Tour of Homes
1st Sunday in December

Tinsel 'N Tidings Craft Fair
3rd Saturday in November

Paris Community Theater
Christmas Performance
*1st and 2nd weekends
in December*

Winter Wonderland,
Bywaters Park
month of December

Christmas in Fairpark
2nd weekend in December

Port Arthur
Greater Port Arthur
Convention and Visitors Bureau
(409) 985-7822 or
(800) 235-7822

Christmas Reflections
month of December

Historic Homes Tour
1st Sunday in December

Arts and Crafts Show
1st weekend in December

Santa Claus Parade and
Ethnic Christmas Celebration
mid-December

Porter
Community Chamber
of Commerce
(281) 348-1531

Christmas Parade
and Tree Lighting
1st Thursday in December

Rusk
Rusk Chamber of Commerce
(903) 683-4242

Christmas Lighting ceremony
December 1

Downtown Christmas Parade
1st Thursday in December

Christmas Tour of Homes
1st Sunday in December

Christmas Readers Theatre
2nd Saturday in December

San Augustine
San Augustine County
Chamber of Commerce
(409) 275-3610

Christmas parade
1st Friday in December

Daughters of the Republic of
Texas Candlelight Tour of Homes
2nd Friday in December

Silsbee
Silsbee Chamber of Commerce
(409) 385-5562

"Christmas in the Big Thicket"
1st Saturday in December

Lighted Christmas Parade
1st Saturday in December

Sugar Land
Annual Nativity Exhibit
at LDS Church
1st weekend in December

CASA Christmas Home Tour
2nd weekend in December

Texarkana
Texarkana B.O.N.D.
(870) 774-2120

Twice As Bright Festival of Lights
*week of Thanksgiving
to January 1*

Tis the Season Yuletide
Celebration
2nd Friday in December

Victorian Christmas
2nd Sunday in December

Tyler
Tyler Area Chamber of Commerce
(903) 592-1661 or
(800) 235-5712

Santa Land
November and December

Wonderland by Night
November and December

Mistletoe and Magic
1st weekend in November

Tyler Jaycees Christmas Parade
1st Thursday in December

Tree Lighting Ceremony
1st Thursday in December

Uncertain
Uncertain Floating Christmas
Parade on Caddo Lake
Sunday before Christmas

Woodville
Candlelight Tour Heritage Village
1st Saturday in December

OTHER ADDRESSES

Camp David B & B
708 West Main Street
Fredericksburg, TX 78624
(830) 997-7797

Cooking With Friends
Jan Bailey
510 Post Oak Road
Fredericksburg, TX 78624
(830) 997-7400

**The DeGolyer House at
The Dallas Arboretum**
8617 Garland Road
Dallas, TX 75218-4332
(214) 327-8263

**Fort Concho National
Historic Landmark**
630 S. Oakes Street
San Angelo, TX 76903-7099
(915) 657-4441

Fredericksburg Herb Farm
402 Whitney
Fredericksburg, TX 78624
(800) 259-HERB

**Fulton Mansion
State Historical Park**
P.O. Box 1859
Fulton, TX 78358
(512) 729-0386

**Galveston Historical
Foundation**
2016 Strand
Galveston, TX 77550-1631
(409) 765-7834

**Gillespie County
Historical Society, Inc.**
312 W. San Antonio St.
Fredericksburg, TX 78624
(830) 997-2835

The Heritage Society
1100 Bagby
Houston, TX 77002-2504
(713) 655-1912

House of the Seasons
P.O. Box 686
Jefferson, TX 75657
(903) 665-1218

The McFaddin-Ward House
1906 McFaddin Avenue
Beaumont, TX 77701
(409) 832-3483

The Range at the Barton House
101 N. Main St.
Salado, TX 76571
(254) 947-3828

Rosevine Inn Bed & Breakfast
415 South Vine
Tyler, TX 75702
(903) 592-2221

**San Antonio
Conservation Society**
107 King William Street
San Antonio, TX 78204
(210) 224-6163

**Sophienburg Museum
& Archives**
200 North Seguin St.
New Braunfels, TX 78130
(830) 629-1900

**Sunrise Rotary
Scholarship Foundation**
P.O. Box 422
Geronimo, TX 78115

Thistle Hill
1509 Pennsylvania Avenue
Fort Worth, TX 76104
(817) 336-1212

Thank You, Texas

Nancy Reynolds
Benjamin Reynolds
Leslie and Brian Reynolds
Marion Szurek
Bob and Nell Shaw
Becky and Ashley Deweese
Ida Castillo
Michael Murphy
Bernie and Sue Ann
   Holtmann
Jane Clancy Debenport
Anice Thompson Vance
Aline Parks
Jennifer Latham
Laurie Covington
George Covington
Emma Gene Schroeder
Dottie Priger
Laura Bush
Betty Higgins
Jodie Gideon
Geoff Walker
Nell Findley
Louise Crocker
Lola Woods
Susan Cottle Leonard
Joe and Eloise Pantalone
Elaine Crane
Doug Beich
Lois Gainer
Ann Mason
Dr. Mickey Bush
Lady Bird Johnson
Dave and Katie Hermann
Lanna Kuehl
Donnie Yeilding
Mary Ware Knudsen
Linda Wilson
Mary Lou Fuller
Eula M. Schmidt
Mildred O. Jenschke
Mary Jane Reeves
Lola Burgess
June Naylor
Joy Graham

Mrs. O. R. Benton
Rebecca Powell
Clarice Hanstrom
Pattizo Humphries
Susan Williams
Marguerite Starr Crain
Melinda Kurz
Ruthie Blair
Ann Buchmann
Ellen Earle
Cindy and Kirby Childress
Matthew White
Ruth Karbach
David Bush
Eve Fleishman
Ann DeBois
Kathy Lee
Lee Wise
Sophienburg Archives
Dorothy Bujnoch
Dr. Rick Barrett
Vlasta Barrett
Debbie Smithdeal
Patti Kimberlin
Bellville Historical Society
Jan Bailey
Gwen and David Fullbrook
Sylvia and William Varney
Anne Rhodes
Pat Carr
Linda Hermes
Dorothy Pechal
Mary Buehring
Sylvia Bonin
Karen Skrivanek
Gladys Kersten
Vernel Bozka
Claudine Ayres
Doris Cardiff
Linda Wilson
Leesa Eklund
V. T. Abercrombie
Richard Grolla
Irma Torres Almager
Pat Schuman

Cassie Sullivan
Chris Schavrda
Sally Sobey
Raoul Nachi
Peggy S. McKay
Lynn Ramsey-Bunton
Karen Gotcher
George Menzies
Andy Wilds
Fulton Mansion
Jewell Ratzlaff
Pansy D. Benedict
Marjorie Otte
Nathan Farr
Santa Claus Museum
Lane Hutchins
Jinny Barnhart
Steve Spain
Genlyn Anderson
William Barney
Gwen Di Stefano
Mary Earney
Peggy Spradley
Page Michel
D. M. Malmsten
Watson Christmas Tree Farm
First Colony Library staff
   Sugar Land
Carol Cummings
Rebecca Watson
Fort Concho
Artie Limmer

Special thanks
to Anne Cook and the
Texas Department of
Transportation for their
generous contribution
of photos and to all the
Visitors' Bureaus and
Chambers of Commerce
around the state for their
assistance.

A TEXAS TASTE TEST

In Texas, we always try to do things bigger and better, so to test the seventy-five recipes submitted for *A Texas Christmas,* Ann Buchmann and Ellen Earle of Sugar Land mobilized the families and friends of Plantation Bend subdivision to participate in a seven-week-long, holiday "Texas Taste-athon." From Thanksgiving to mid-January, our hardworking cooks and bakers whipped up gastronomic delights for neighborhood coffees, supper clubs, family gatherings, Bible study groups, ladies' club meetings, and even a pecan tasting party. Roughly 50 pounds of pecans later, the results are in, and collective "raves" go to Pecan Tassies, Mama Lou's Banana Nut Cake, and Deep, Dark Chocolate Cake in the "Sweets" category; Spinach Madeleine and Mogen David Salad in the "Christmas Feast" category; and Feta Cheese Dip and Armadillo Eggs share the kudos for "Party Fare."

Many thanks to Ann Buchmann and Ellen Earle and their crew of willing cooks and bakers who gave our neighborhood the tastiest holiday season ever!

THE COOKS AND BAKERS
Ann Buchmann, Ellen Earle, Lauren Goonan, Stephen and Sheila Simmons Schubarth, Pam Goodfriend, Melinda Kurz, Laurie Covington, George Covington, Marilyn Covington, Ruthie Blair, Sandy Kelly, Mary Knudsen, Sharon Pierson, Laurie Levin, and Maureen McClure.

THE TASTERS
Martha Cantrell, Carolyn and Max Williams, Pat Mehta, Bill and Sharon Sole, Bob and Judy Mileff, Rob Mileff, Rick and Ann Buchmann, Andy Buchmann, Mark Buchmann, Bob and Heather Bobo, Robert and Maggie Redding, Brandon and Patsy Stewart, Doug and Ellen Earle, Ida Earle, Kara Earle, Lewis and Yvonne Ware, Bob and Kim Stratton, Lindy LeBert, Velma LeBert, Joan and Harry Shattuck, Maureen and Derek McClure, Paul and Lee Pierson, Chris and Nancy Pierson, Sharon and Neil Pierson, Marcelle Pierson, Michael and Mary Knudsen, Charlotte and Leonard Earle, Dan and Hanna MacDonald, Grace and German Amador, George and Marilyn Covington, Laurie Covington, Emily Levin, Laurie Levin, Afshan Kaviani, Keitha Robinson, Letty Albright, Sandy and Chris Kelly, Debbie Jones, Chris Schneider, Ruthie Blair, Amy Lewis, Carol and Reinder de Boer, Sylvia Farmer, Ashley Fuller, Casee Blakley, Rick and Waynette Fuller, Kristyn Fuller, Kitty and Tom Vann, Helen and Edward Iyadi, Keith Blair, Rebekah Blair, Paul Blair, Melinda and Ken Kurz, Mike and Pam Goodfriend, Lauren and Brian Goonan, Stephen and Sheila Simmons Schubarth, Liz Nicolichuk, Pauline Vickers, Norman Kent, Judith Farrow, Gib Crunk, Rose Warren, Todd Brown, and Barry Boyse.

PHOTO CREDITS